AROUND
FAREHAM

From Old Photographs

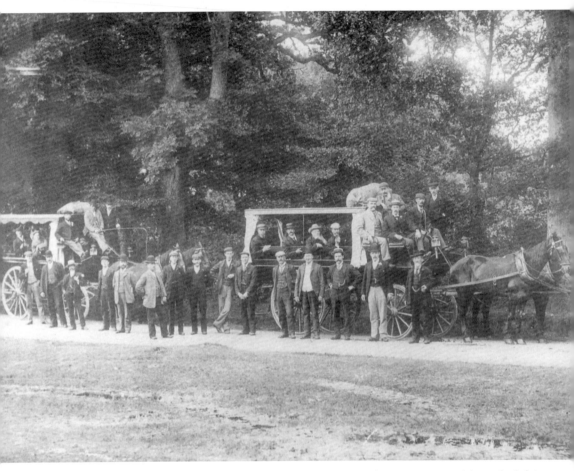

A group planning a Sunday trip to Warsash for a 'Crab and Lobster Tea'. Second from the left is Mr Misselbrook, third is Mr See, fifth Mr Latty, sixth Mr W. H. Chance, seventh and eighth are his sons, tenth is Mr A. Chance and twelfth is Mr Ruffey. This picture seems very apt to begin a book entitled *Around Fareham*.

AROUND FAREHAM

From Old Photographs

ALICE JAMES

AMBERLEY

First published by Tempus Publishing Limited, 1998
This edition published 2009

Copyright © The Estate of Alice James 2009

Amberley Publishing
Cirencester Road, Chalford,
Stroud, Gloucestershire, GL6 8PE

British Library Cataloguing in Publication Data.
A catalogue record for this book is available from the British Library.

ISBN 978 1 84868 612 0

Typesetting and origination by Amberley Publishing
Printed in Great Britain

To the members, past and present, of the Fareham Local History Group.

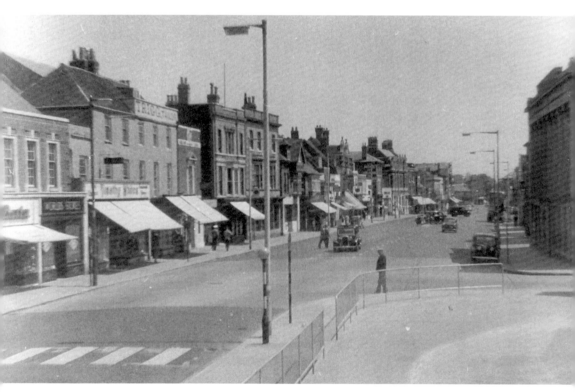

West Street in 1955 – 'wide enough for cars to park in the middle' (*Fareham Urban District Guide*, 1965).

Contents

Acknowledgements

The greater number of these images come from my very large collection of cards and photographs, gathered over many years. However, I should also like to acknowledge contributions of material and information from the following:

Messrs Aylott, Baxandall, Binns, Bliss, Elphick, Esser, Evans, Ford, Goodall, Grant, Hahn, Hoare, Holmes, Knipe, Maude-Roxby, Palk, Perry, Softly, Tame, Waring, Whyte. Mesdames Barton, Billett, Bishop, Clapperton, Colwell, Cooper, Edds, Etherington, Foss, Le Tissier and Wright. Photographers who are no longer with us include, Messrs Brown, Crouch and Privett. I would also like to thank The London Camera Exchange, Fareham Planning Dept., Westbury Manor Museum and Studio 6. Last, but not least, I thank my husband, who kept on typing in spite of everything.

Further Reading

G. Privett, *The Story of Fareham*
R. Aylott (and A. James), *Fareham: Two Views*
R. A. Stone, *The Mean Valley Railway*
J. Emery, *Fareham in Old Picture Postcards*
A. James, *Fareham between the Wars*
P. Moore, *Bygone Fareham*
A. James, *Our Beloved Fareham*
L. Burton and B. Musselwhite, *An Illustrated History of Fareham*
R. Brown, *Stubbington and Titchfield*
A. James, *Fareham*

Introduction

In my last book, *Fareham*, published by the Chalford Publishing Company [known today as Tempus Publishing] in 1996, I bewailed the fact that I could not include some of the outlying areas, such as Wallington, Knowle and Fontley, and hoped that it might be possible to write a book called 'Outside Fareham'. With a slight change of title here it is.

Already in the last two years there have been many changes in central Fareham and its surroundings and so this is an attempt to record some of those changes. The redevelopment of the Precinct in the heart of old Fareham and the proposed development of the Market Site and land south of West Street will inevitably mean that some of this book will be out of date by the time that it is published! In this second selection, we are venturing further afield to take in some of the old villages and settlements now considered to be part of Fareham Borough, but which both historically and in modern times still retain their own identities – even if they are becoming swamped with new housing.

Fontley, once with its brick and tile industries, the products of which (along with those from Fareham Common) literally went all over the world, is now largely residential. Its old iron industry is claimed by Fareham giving it a lost identity. Wallington, once noted for its tannery, brewery, brick and tile works, is now much given over to residential areas, although there have been developments in light industry together with a large supermarket. Then there is the loss of Knowle Hospital with the present threat of 800 houses, light industrial development and a road across farmland to the A32 near Albany Farm – which already has light industrial development. When Professor Colin Buchanan's plan for a Solent City was rejected there was some relief. Now, this seems to be 'happening by stealth', as a resident of Fontley said to me. There has been a steady but remorseless advance of housing and modern business centres. Farmland is disappearing to be inevitably replaced by roads and traffic as businesses set up in old farm buildings. Out of town shopping has helped to swamp areas, such as Segensworth, as large supermarkets develop and old shopping centres suffer.

There does appear to be a certain revival of interest in town centres that I hope will continue. To quote from the *Fareham Urban District Guide* of 1965: 'Fareham is fortunate in having a main shopping street wide enough to provide for a car park down the centre, a factor which has contributed to the business of the town. The shops and pavements provide everything to encourage people to enjoy their shopping expeditions. The shop buildings are of good design and well maintained [...] and shopping can be enjoyed in the spirit of friendliness, a feeling that there is good value for money and that the trade of the town is alive'. However, we have lost such shops as Dodges, Philips,

Burts and Waters (to name a few) to the Precinct. West Street is now pedestrianised and some people think that it is now rather bleak. New plans are being evolved but they will bring back West Street – once one of the finest Hampshire main roads – as one of the narrowest roads in the county.

Thankfully, there are still wide-open areas and settlements to enjoy even though some country lanes have become routes for through traffic and walking is not advocated. I have tried to include some of these, together with some of the large country houses, in this second selection.

There are 226 photographs in this book, eighty-five of which were taken in 1998. I must acknowledge the help of many other photographers past and present. I hope older people will remember and younger people might be encouraged to look around. It is an area where I have lived for the greater part of my life and which I regard with so much affection despite any changes, which after all, I suppose, are bound to come as a result of a changing world.

Alice James
1998

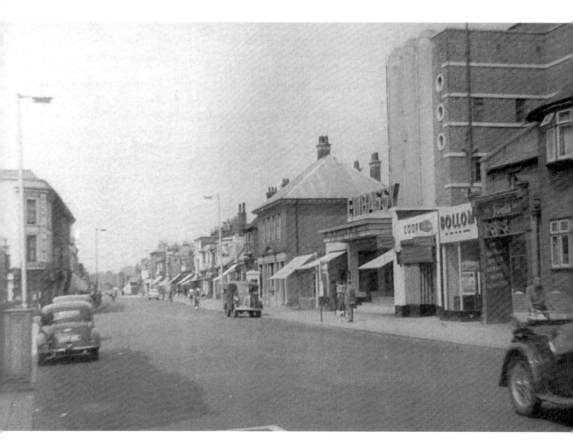

West Street in 1955. The Embassy cinema and the dentist's house on the corner have long gone.

One

Fareham Town

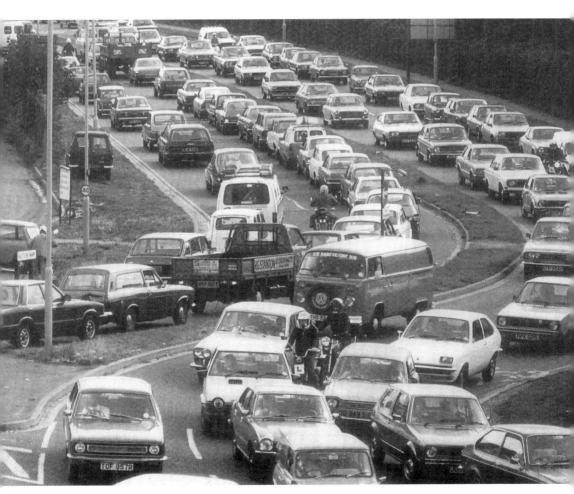

Fareham's problem – traffic! This photograph was taken in 1981 on Eastern Way near the Gosport/Fareham roundabout.

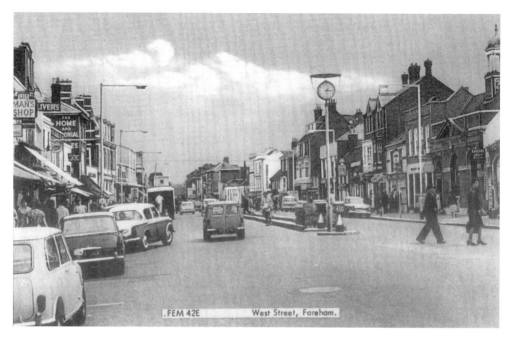

West Street in 1965. This was taken prior to any changes, when the street was full of good shops and parking was still possible.

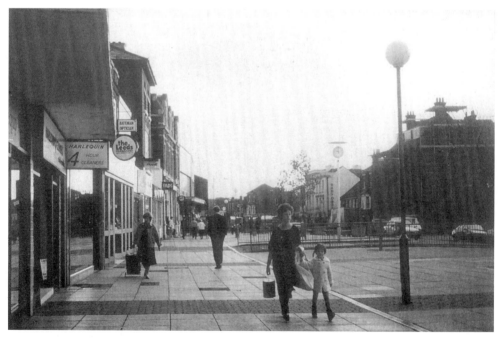

The same area in 1990, having been pedestrianised by 1982. An interesting comment in *A Vision of the Future* (1998) is that it is 'at present looking a little sad and unremarkable' – Farehamites have always said so.

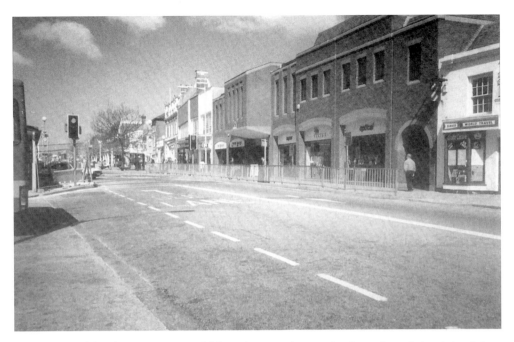

The outside of the shopping centre, which underwent changes that 'were intended to bring it into the next millennium'.

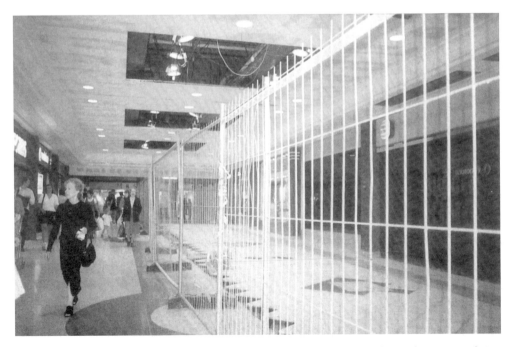

Taken in 1998, this photograph shows that refurbishment had started. This is the entrance being re-floored.

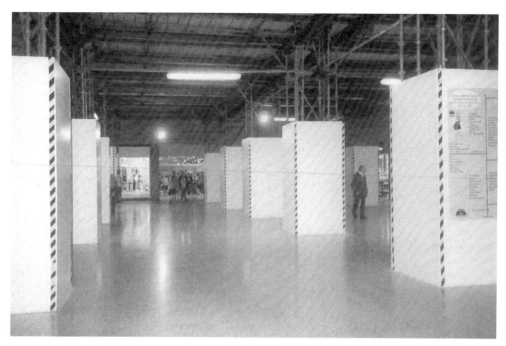

At the time of this photograph, roofs were being raised, natural light let in and a new entrance developed.

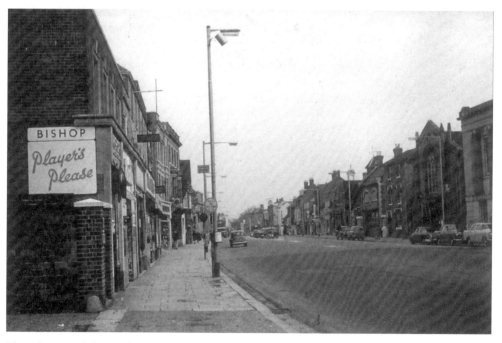

This photograph lets us look back with nostalgia to 1962 when people's needs were catered for and 'shopping was enjoyed in a spirit of friendliness'.

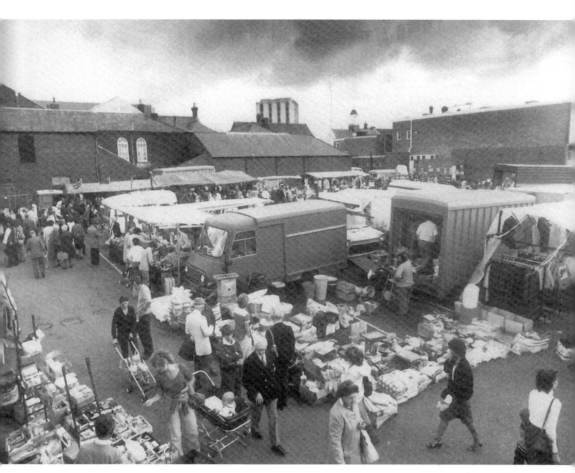

In this picture from 1998, the old cattle market has long gone. Since this picture was taken, the market site has been redeveloped. From being one of the widest streets in Hampshire, pedestrianised West Street became the narrowest.

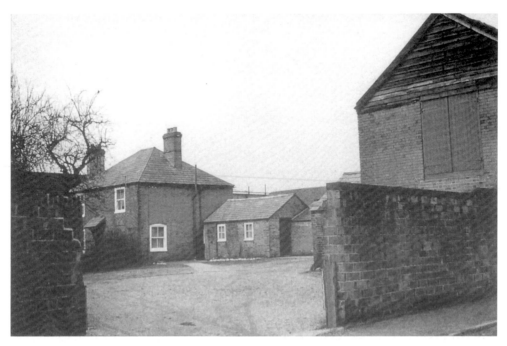

Westbury Farm, 1962. These buildings lay alongside Westbury path but were destroyed by vandals in 1996.

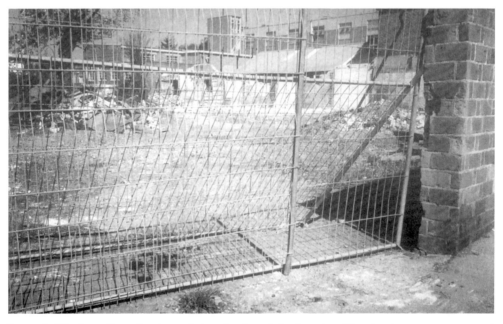

In 1998, Westbury Farm land was being developed for housing. The development was named after Admiral Moresby who 'discovered' Papua New Guinea. Port Moresby was named after him.

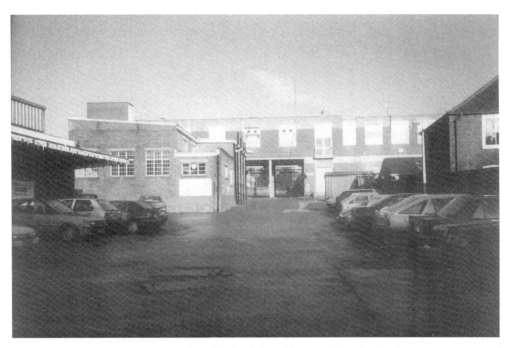

Extending back from Westbury path and behind the old post office, this land is a continuation of the land shown in the previous picture.

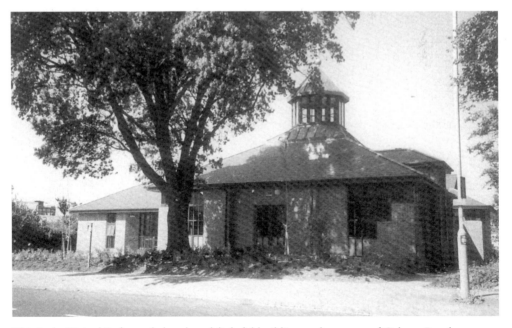

This is the United Reformed church, a delightful building at the corner of Osborn Road.

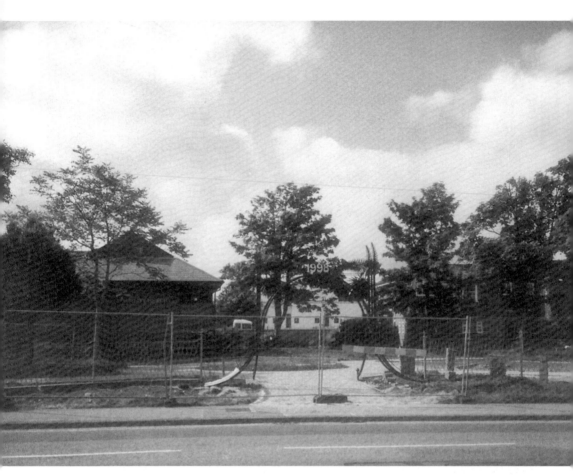

This is the site of another change. The grassy slopes, trees and flowerbeds near the United Reformed church have gone to make a memorial garden for Diana, Princess of Wales. It is primarily for the visually impaired with well-laid-out paths. We know the excellence of Fareham Council's gardeners and only hope that the work will not be spoilt by skate-boarders or rollerbladers. The memorial garden was completed in September 1998 and Fareham was the first town in Hampshire to complete its garden.

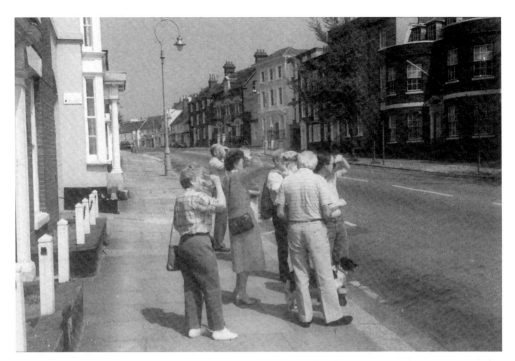

The (relatively unchanging) high street with a few interested sightseers.

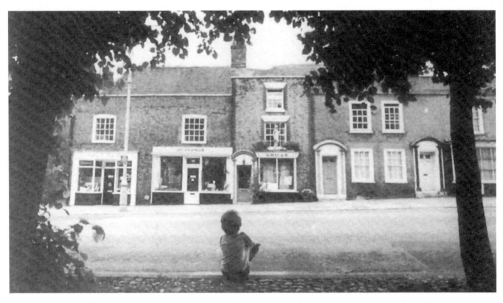

Looking towards No. 13 to No. 17 High Street. There have been some wonderful discoveries at No. 15 (Chives) by its owner, Mr H. A. Palk, who found that the exterior masked the true medieval interior and that the house in fact dates from 1294. There are twelve separate rooms in the two properties, which are joined into one entity. No two rooms are on the same level and there is always a staircase to negotiate.

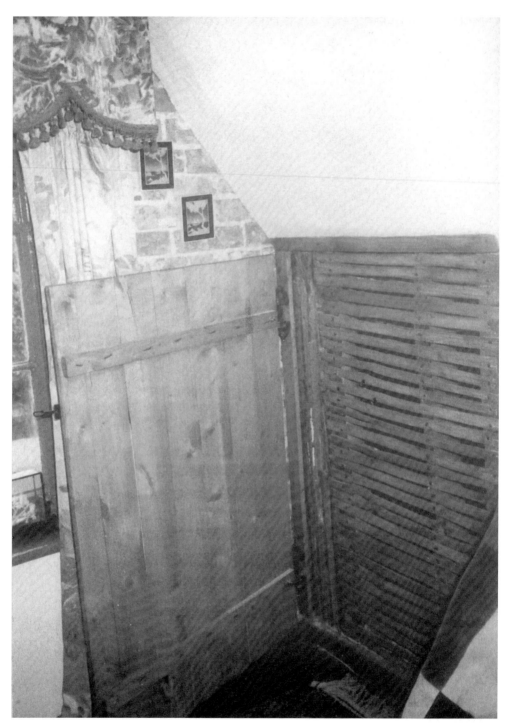

This shows the original wattle-and-daub wall. It has been possible to check the timbers using dendrochronology and the house is graded at Grade II*. The 'new' Georgian roof now encapsulates the original roof.

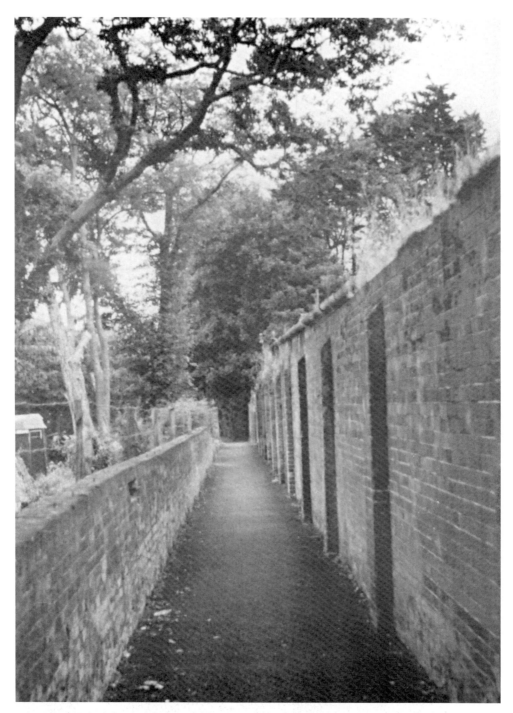

Lysses Path, which leads from the high street to Bridgefoot (now the large Delmé roundabout). When excavations took place at Portchester Castle, it was found that the original gateway was directly in line with the Roman Way and the bottom of Bridgefoot, where there was once a bridge now hidden under the roundabout.

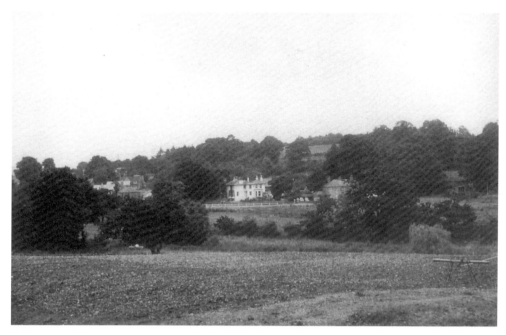

The view from Lysses Path, looking towards Wallington, before the residential settlement was developed. This was taken in 1964.

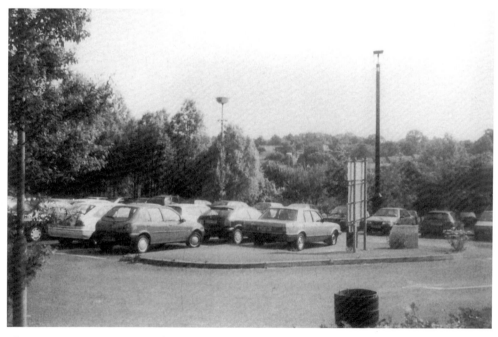

The same view in 1998. A very large car park now extends down to Wallington Way.

Two

Wallington Village

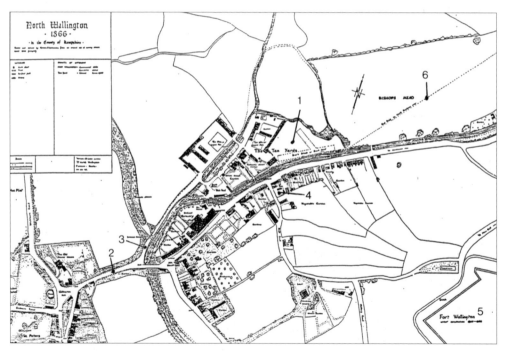

A copy of an old map dated 1866. It shows the old village with:

1. Extensive tan yards
2. Wallington Hill
3. Broadcut
4. Saunder's Brewery
5. Fort Wallington – 'under construction'
6. The footpath to North Fareham, which links up through to Pool Lane and with the A32.

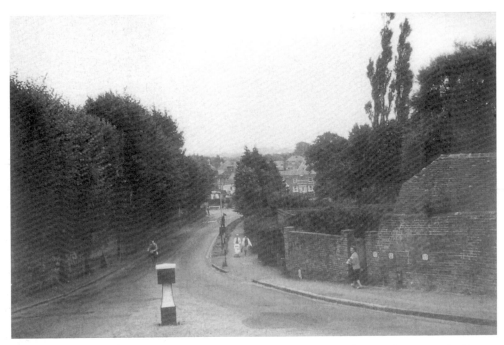

The old route to Wallington was by Wallington Hill, a very steep slope and a terror for learner drivers!

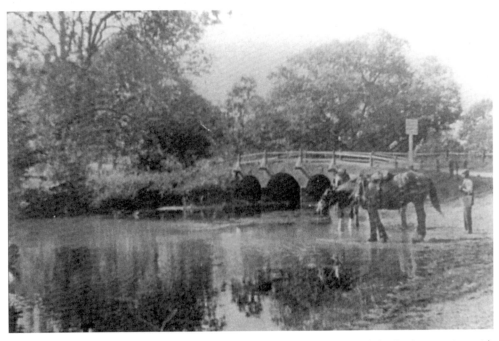

At the bottom of the hill is old Broadcut, with the River Wallington and the ford across it – with a gap so the horses could be watered.

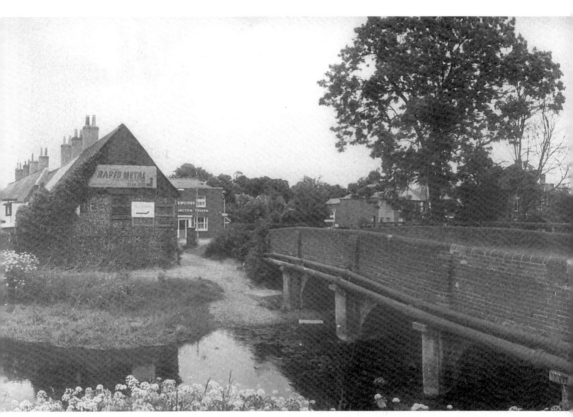

This shows the old bridge and the ford across the river. Cottages and sheds have been pulled down and modern houses have grown up. The pub, still unaltered, is the Fort Wallington Tavern. Above the bridge was a nesting place for two swans, known as George and Margaret, which were later to result in the pub being renamed the 'Cob and Pen' in 1984.

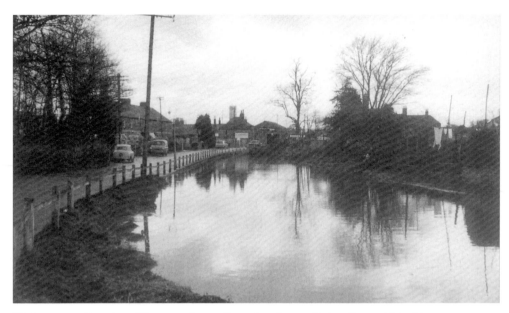

High water at Broadcut. The water is receding after the road's flooding at high tide.

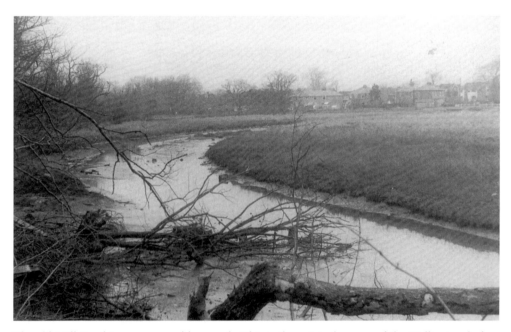

The old Mill Pond is now covered by marsh. This is the original course of the Wallington before it was diverted and the roundabout built.

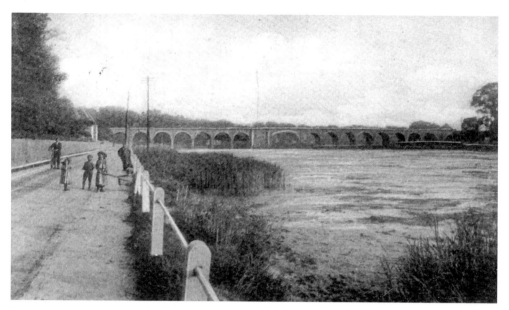

This is the old road from the Delmé Arms to Wallington. The extent of the Mill Pond is clearly visible.

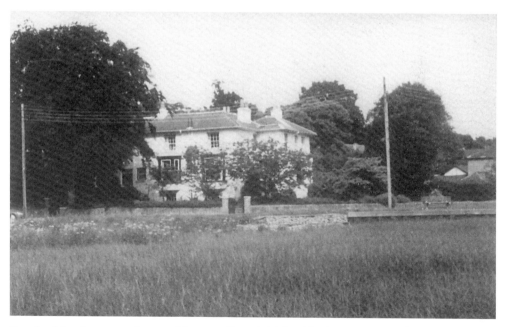

'Lowlands' – the present home of Surgeon Captain Hahn. The house was carefully sited to avoid possible floods. It was built in 1832 and was once known as Wallington Cottage.

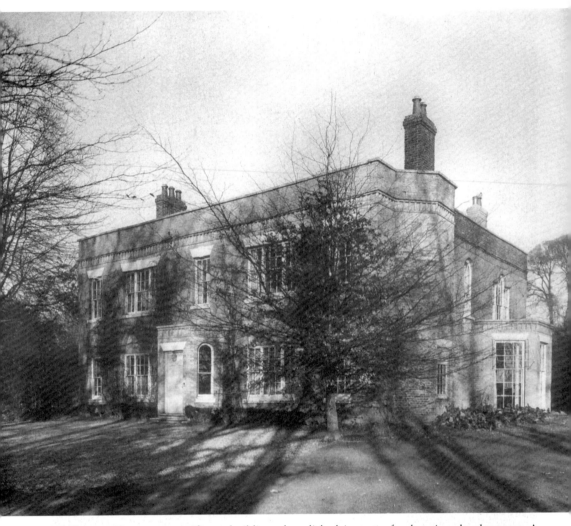

Wallington House, a magnificent building, demolished in 1967 for housing development. A protest to the young man in the then planning office resulted in the answer that it was 'of no architectural merit'. For many years, it was held by the War Office, but finally became the home of the Coppinger family. Doctor Coppinger went, in HMS *Discovery*, to the Arctic on the Nares Polar Expedition in 1876. His descendants lived on in the house until the 1960s.

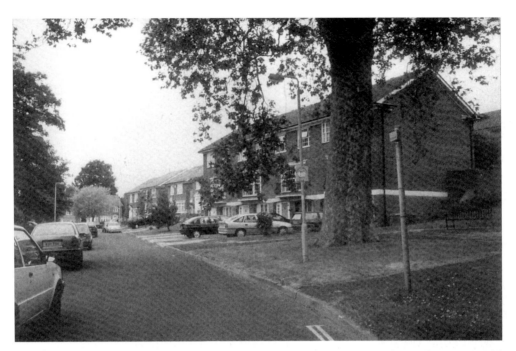

Taking the place of Wallington House is a housing estate of which Waterside Gardens is a typical *cul de sac*.

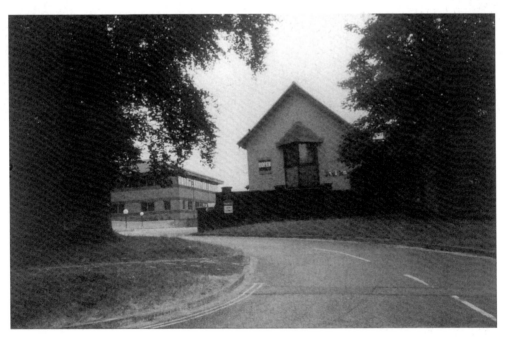

The spare grassland with its pleasant trees was inevitably taken over by developers, in spite of village protests.

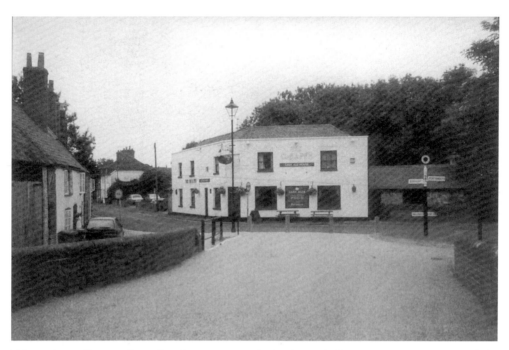

Taking the Wallington Shore Road, we come to the bridge and the junction. Here is situated the Cob and Pen, which commemorates the two original swans, George and Margaret.

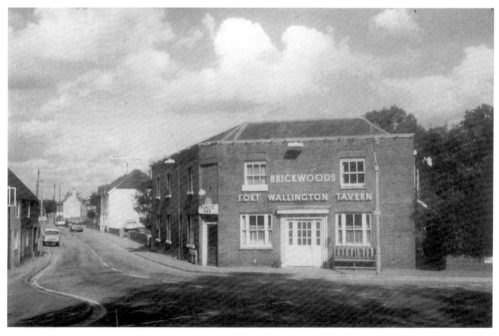

The pub was originally called the Fort Wallington Tavern and did much to supply the needs of the garrison at Fort Wallington.

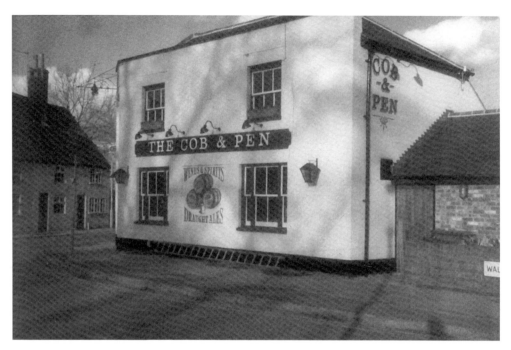

Closed for three years for alterations, the pub reopened in 1984 with its new name.

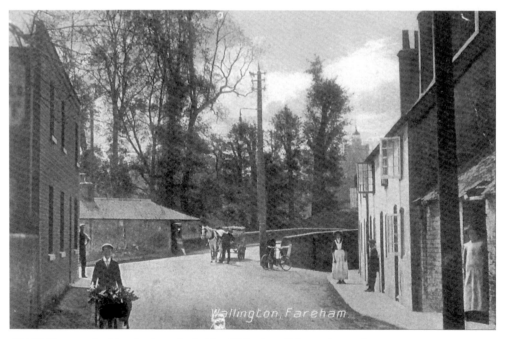

Old Wallington, looking back to the bridge. This view did not change for many years.

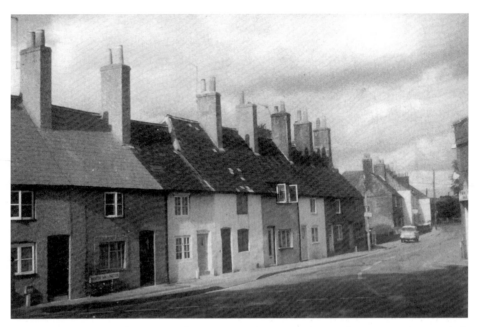

The same cottages in the 1960s, of which some have now been taken over and gentrified. Those nearer the bridge are still liable to flooding.

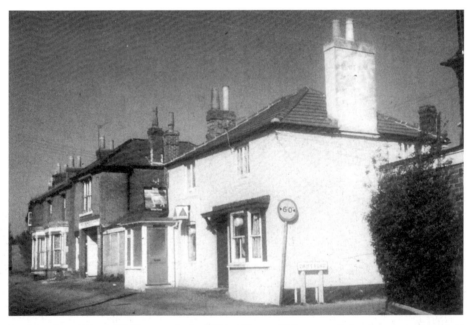

Further along North Wallington is the White Horse. This part of the river is well looked after, with gardens at the side, and populated with ducks and fish to make a pleasant region. Drift Road, an old drover's road, joins North Wallington and on it is the old brewery, now a residential area.

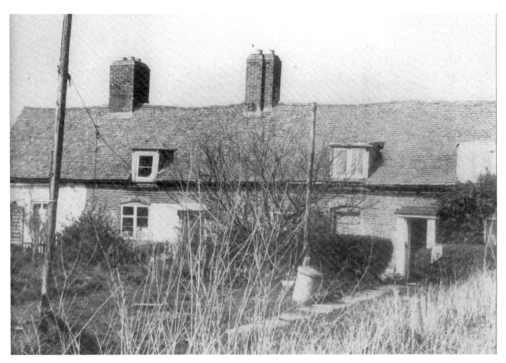

Although Drift Road is now built up, some of the old cottages remain.

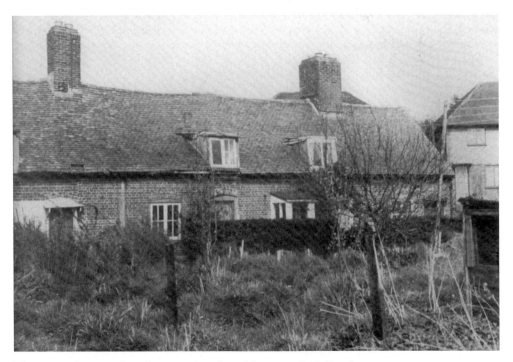

These two photographs, taken together, show Nos 2-10, Drift Road.

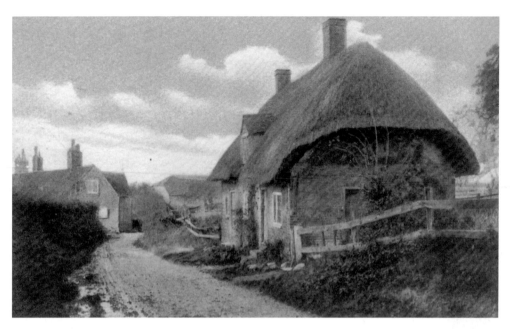

Looking back down Drift Road. The thatched cottages still remain but the road has now been considerably improved and is now built up.

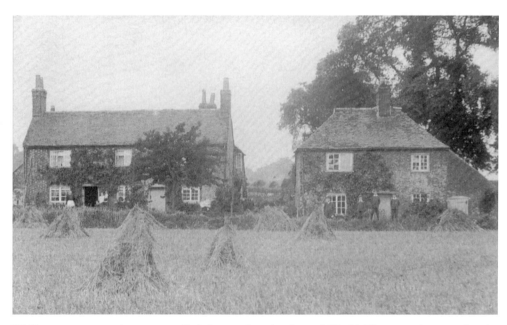

Wallington cottages that were pulled down after the Second World War to make way for the industrial estate.

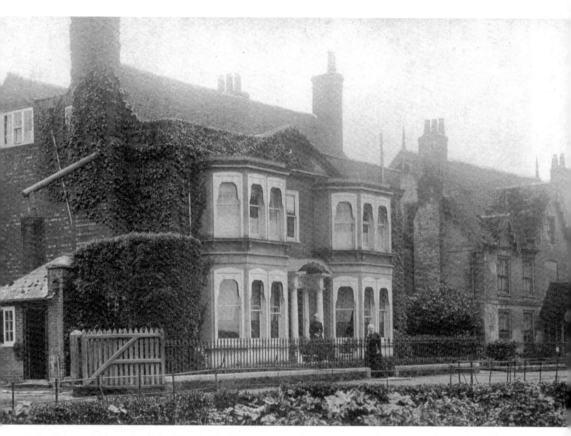

Lying between Broadcut and North Wallington were the tanneries, which dominated the life of Wallington. There are records of tanneries going back to the time of Charles I. This is Purvestor House, the home of (the then owner) Mr Sharland. There was a magnificent garden and it was possible to cut through by the side of the house to reach Broadcut. We are fortunate in having a complete family record of the area and the works. The house next door belonged to Mr Brown and was supposedly haunted. The tanneries gave much work both to Wallington and North Fareham and, although it closed before the Second World War, it is still in the memories of some old Wallingtonians. The daughters, Miss Emily and Miss Mary Jane, are particularly well remembered. Mrs Sharland was nicknamed 'Queen Victoria' and Mr Sharland was a tower of strength to St Peter and Paul's church, saving it from fire damage by organising soaking wet hides on the roof when the barn of Fareham Farm caught fire.

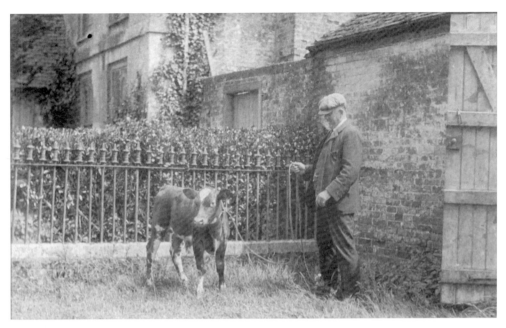

There was also a farm at the tanneries together with a dairy. All employees were given a quart of skimmed milk daily.

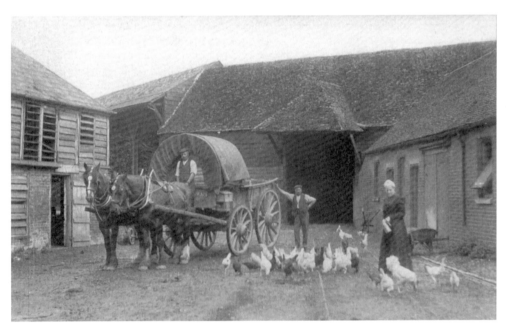

Behind the tan yards where the bark was stored. This picture shows Mr and Mrs Evans in the farmyard.

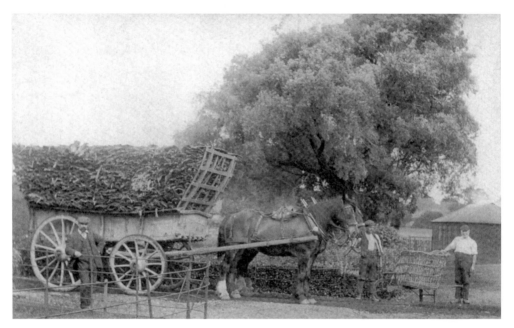

Collecting the bark harvest. Mr Holman is the carter.

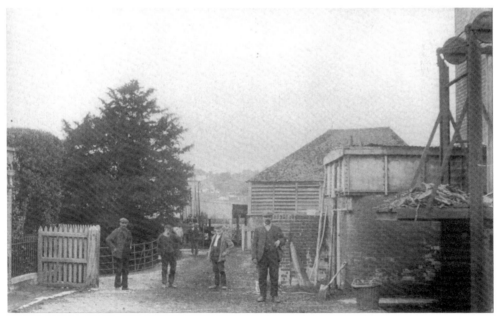

The spent bark can be seen on the left, with the tan pit building on the right. Hides are being lifted into the pits. Mr Harris is on the left and on the right is Mr Morris, the tan pit manager.

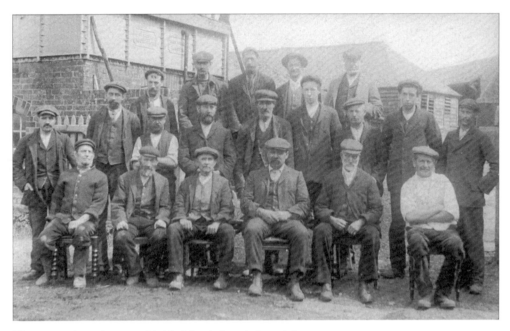

The tan yard employees, with Mr Morris fourth from left.

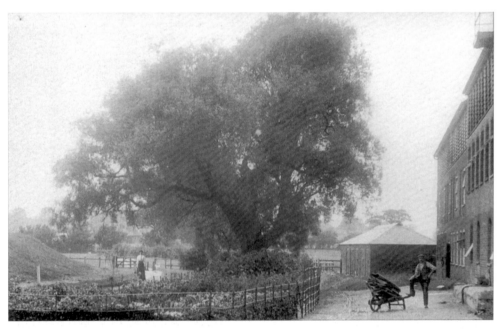

This shows the spent tan bark on the left, the tan pit building on the right and a worker with rolled hides on his cart. The smaller building apparently had something to do with steam generation. This photograph provides a first glimpse of Miss Emily!

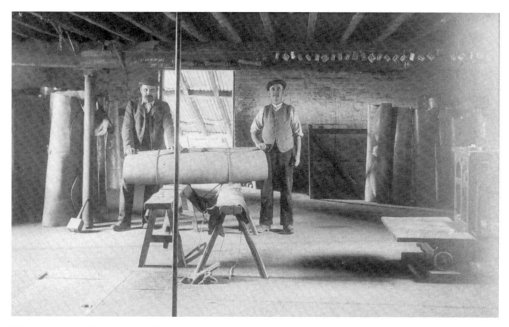

The completed leather – rolled, baled and tied with a 'tan yard knot'. This was apparently a double reef knot.

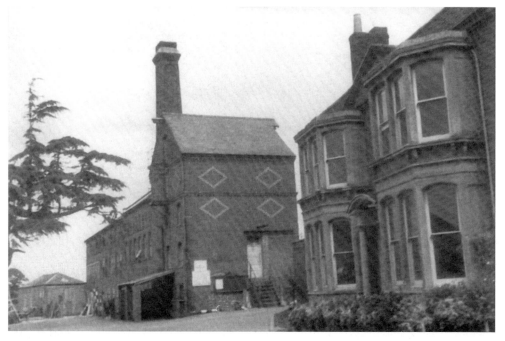

The closed tannery building and empty Purvestor House. The house was occupied during the Second World War by the AFS, ARP and ambulance service. Fire practices were held here.

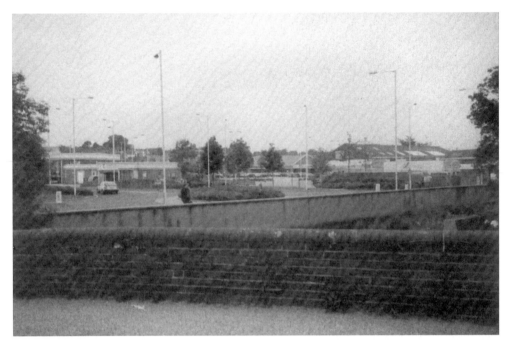

Broadcut with the river tamed between high walls and a large Sainsbury's store and other warehouses. This now leads to an extensive industrial area covering the tan yard site and beyond, with the loss of the water meadows.

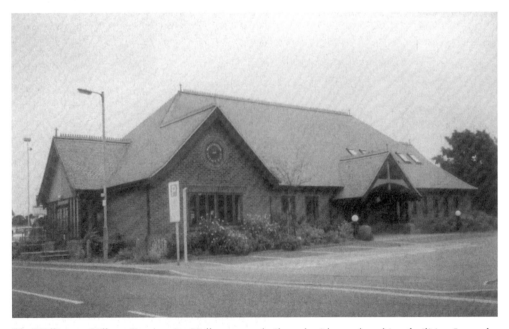

The Wallington Village Community Hall, purpose-built and with good parking facilities. It can be reached from the White Horse area by a footbridge, which marks high tide limit on the river.

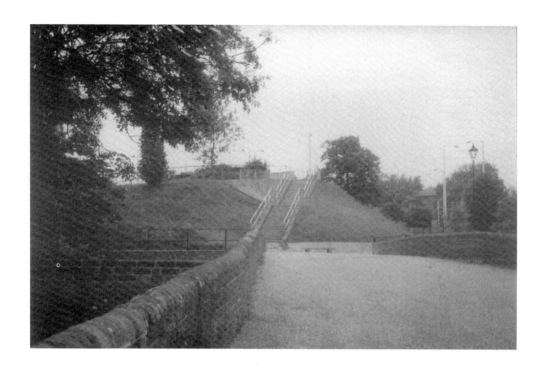

Above: The old bridge leading to the pedestrian bridge over Wallington Way. There is also a sloping path, although neither are particularly helpful to the elderly.

Right: Opening of Wallington Village Hall, 1995. Mr Perry presents a bouquet to WVCA's oldest member, Mrs Kitty Hines. The youngest member, Laura Swinburn, sits on the floor, waiting for her turn to be presented with a posy. She was then thirteen months old.

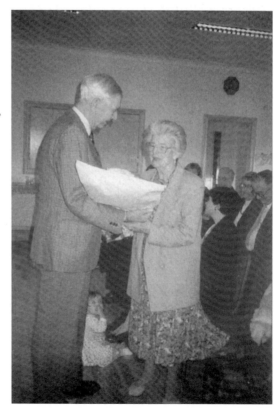

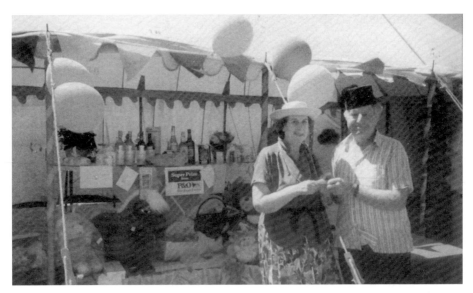

Village fête, 1990. Howard and Dyliss Draper are working the tombola.

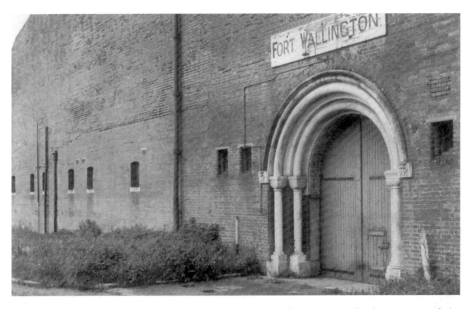

Fort Wallington is one of the land forts set up by Palmerston in the latter part of the nineteenth century. It was at one time garrisoned by Irish troops who provided work (in the form of laundry) to the women of Wallington. Fort Wallington Tavern catered for other needs! At one point there was a boys' school, the Gordon Academy. Its importance declined and it came under private ownership. One eccentric owner actually declared UDI from Fareham Council and there was an attempt by him to blow up part of it. He was taken to court by nearby residents who objected to flying bricks. There was also a 'Dungeon Club' advertising meals in the seventeenth-century dungeons – despite the fort being of nineteenth-century construction. It is now, rather prosaically, an industrial estate.

Three

Old Turnpike to Knowle

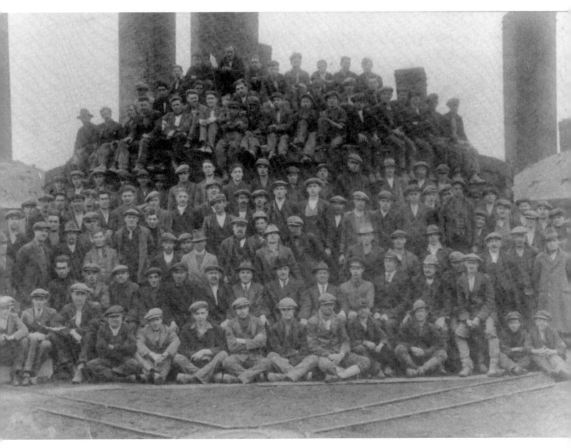

Fontley Brick and Tile Works. This boasted a workforce of 260 men and boys plus one dog!

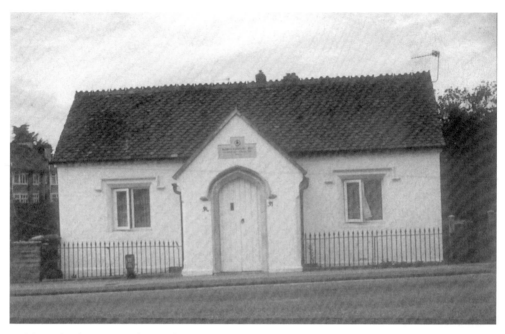

Paddon Almshouses on the Wickham Road. They were built by Mr Paddon in memory of his mother and provide a home for two ladies.

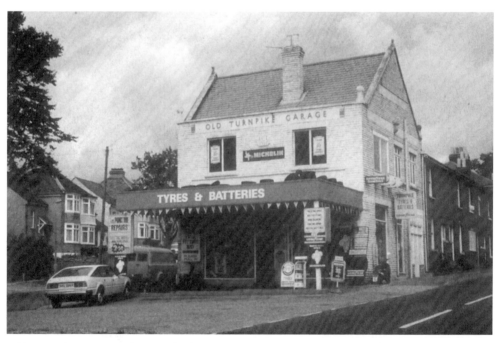

Old Turnpike garage. This was built from the stones that were rejected for First World War memorial use: they must conceal much past history. The original tollgates were located here.

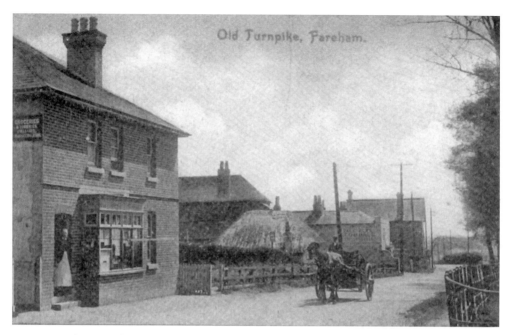

Here, near the top of Old Turnpike, is the old New Inn, which was to be replaced later by the New Inn! It was always in the hands of the Goodall family. It is now renamed the Turnpike.

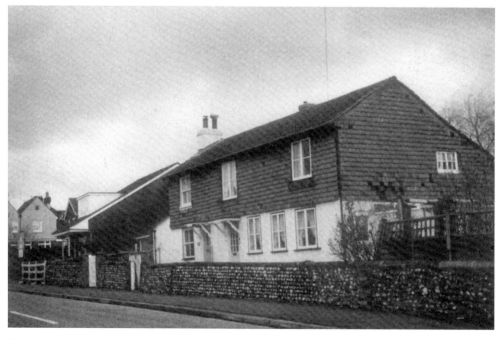

Pipe workers' cottages on Old Turnpike. There was a thriving clay-pipe-making industry in this region, the Goodall family being the most important people in the business. Note the old cattle pound between the cottages and the New Inn.

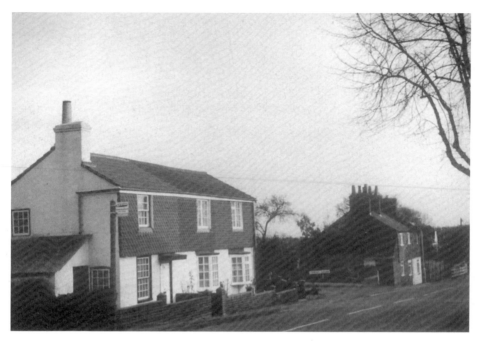

More delightful cottages. A road leading to a more modern housing estate has now breached their line.

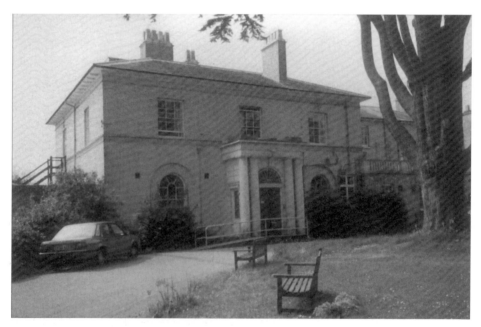

Uplands House, once the home of Samuel Jellicoe, later of John Beardmore and latterly of Captain Miller. Jellicoe, a naval paymaster, was found guilty of defrauding the government and was declared bankrupt. His partner, Henry Cart, was beggared as a result. Beardmore had a fine collection of armour, which is now in London.

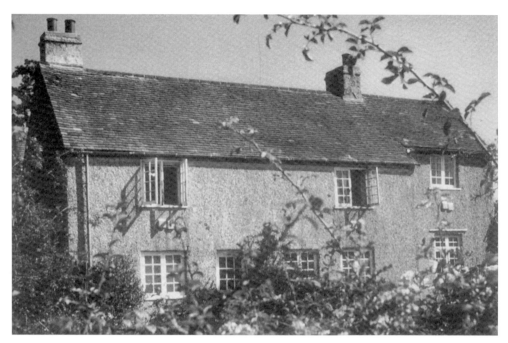

Kneller Cottages. Continuing along Kiln Road, past Maylings Farm Road, we come to a narrow, steep lane with lodges, which is the entrance to Kneller Court. At the bottom are Kneller Cottages.

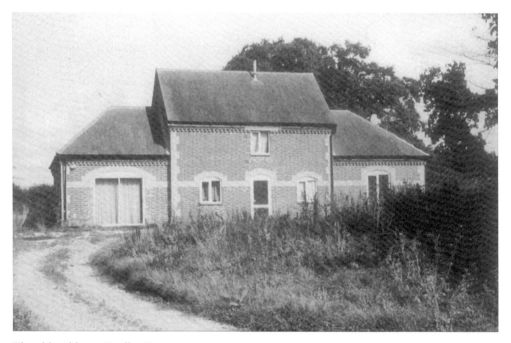

The old stables at Kneller Court.

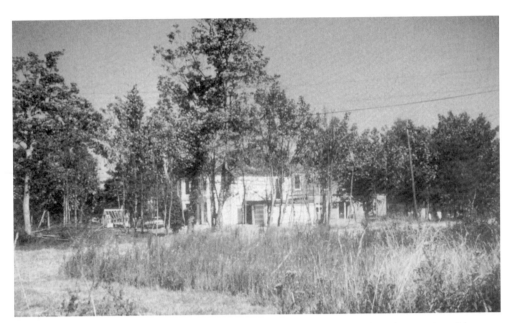

Kneller Court itself, as seen from the cottages. It has been much altered, in spite of its age, probably because it was completely hidden from the road. The home of the Kneller family, court painters, it has a reputation for being haunted.

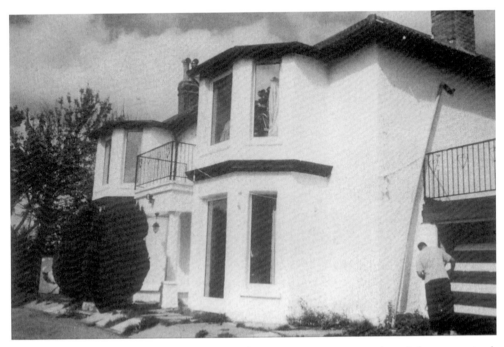

The front of Kneller Court. The whole area has given rise to many tales of the paranormal, indeed, far too many to be dismissed lightly. Even the author got involved in a time warp and was not alone at the time!

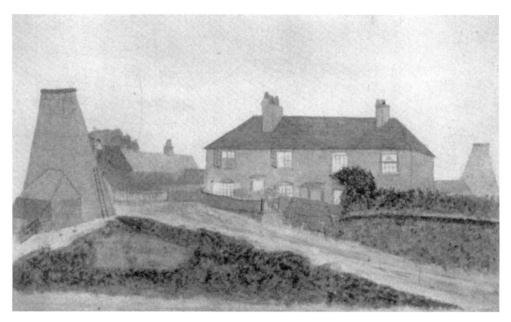

Holly Grove and kilns at the turn of the century. It must be remembered that all Kiln Road had brick industries. The clay for the Fareham Reds was found in what is now known as Green Hollow Close in Highlands Road. Fareham Reds have not been made for many years.

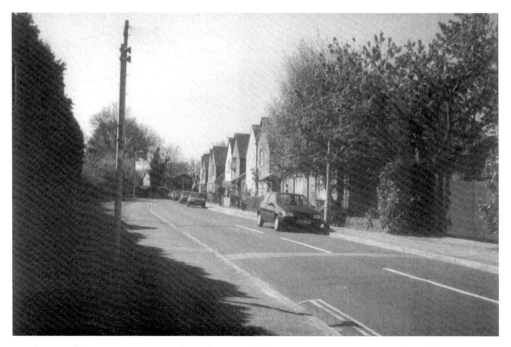

Modern Holly Grove, now a residential area and, like Kiln Road, plagued with traffic.

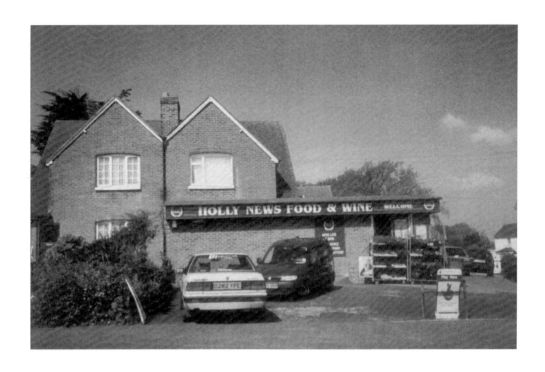

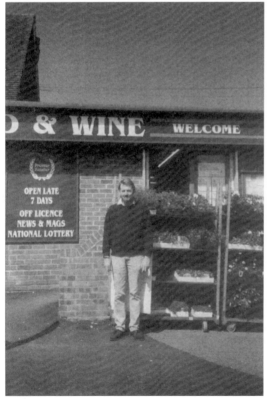

Above: Holly stores at the junction of Fontley Road, Kiln Road, Holly Grove and Red Barn Lane.

Left: Mr C. Price, proprietor of the Holly stores. The plants and the notice on the wall tell of his hard work. Inside, he sells groceries and, in 1998, he added 'post office' to the list.

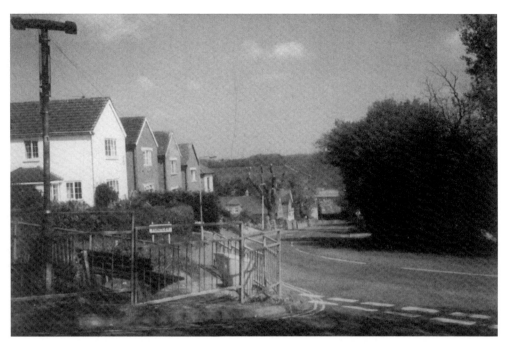

The top of Fontley Road, looking down Fontley Hill. All of this area is now heavily residential.

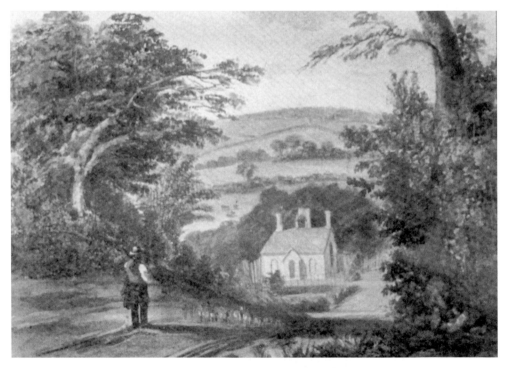

Old Fontley church, dedicated to St Francis. Note the absence of housing.

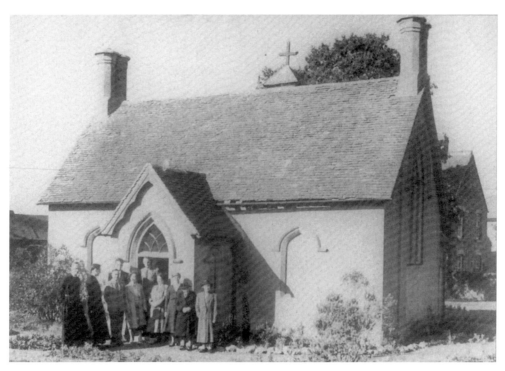

The church when the Revd A. Watkins was vicar. It is attached to SS Peter and Paul and celebrated its centenary in 1956.

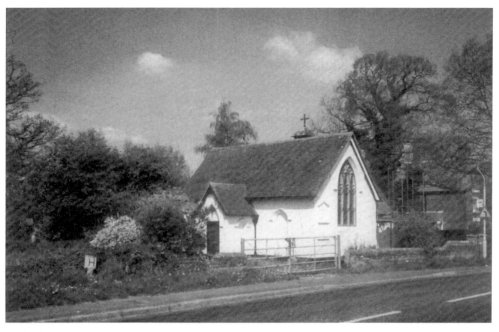

The church in 1998, with its famous Ruskin window. Well cared for, it is over 150 years old.

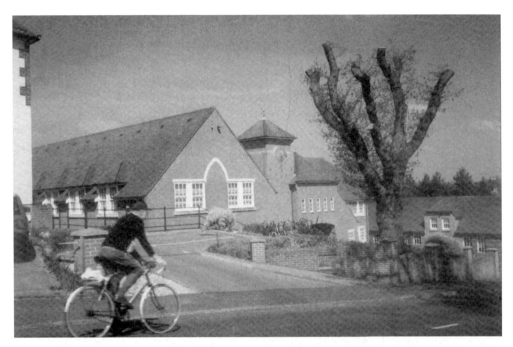

The present school, also on Fontley Hill.

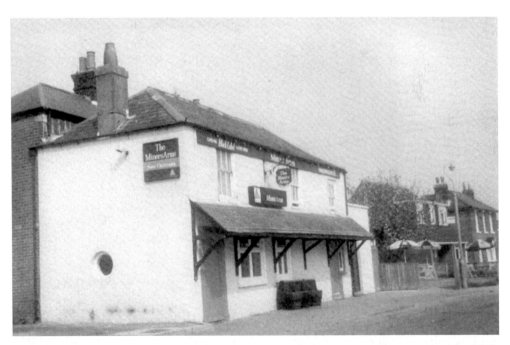

Going down to the main village, the Miners Arms lies almost opposite the great Brick and Tile Works. Workers, who were engaged in constructing the new railway line, named the pub. The works area is now swallowed up by development but a large ornamental lake has been created from the great claypit. Beside it is 'Lakeside'.

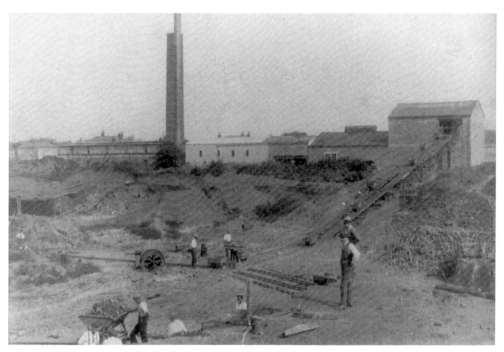

The great clay pit at the works with the continuous kiln. The great boiler house chimney was 110 feet high.

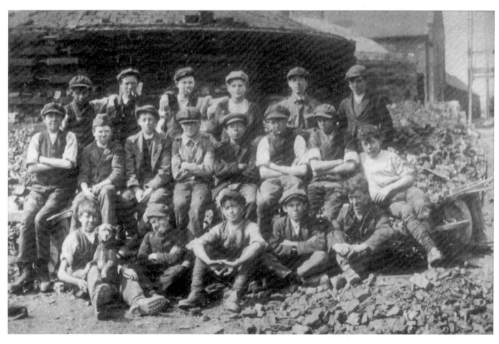

Boys at the works, along with the dog. They were employed as tilers, oil boys, press operators and sanders. Note that at least four are smoking!

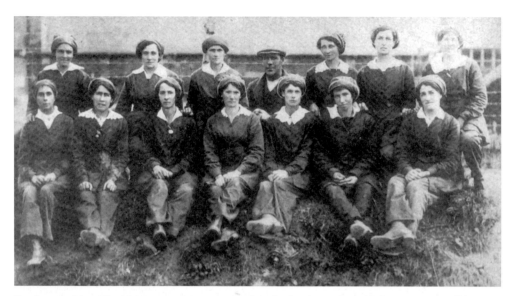

During the First World War, cordite was stored at the brick works and these women, all bar one from Fontley, worked there. They are, from left to right, back row: Mrs Hoare, Mrs Ship, Mrs Carter, Mrs Jukes, Mrs Newby and Mrs Harris. Front row: Mrs Smith, Mrs Fletcher, Mrs Hoad, Mrs Akers, Mrs Jones, Mrs Crouch and Mrs Randall. The foreman is Harry Waters; note the heavy boots.

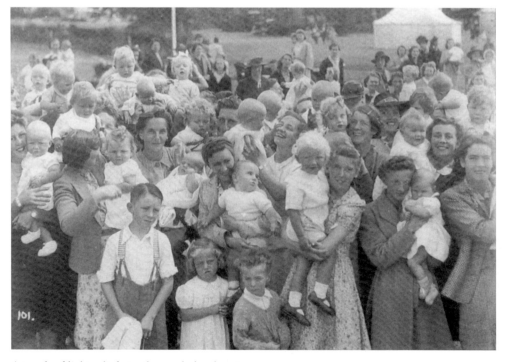

A touch of light relief at a 'bonny baby show'.

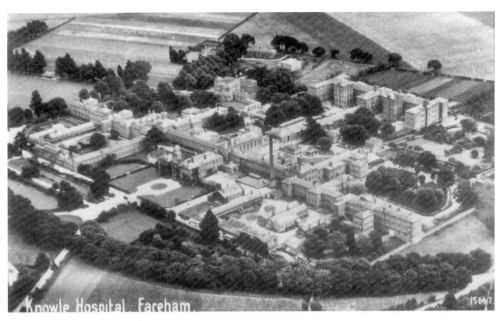

Continuing along the road and over the railway bridge we come to Knowle Hospital, shown here from the air. Now demolished, it was always known for its excellent care. Several generations of families worked there.

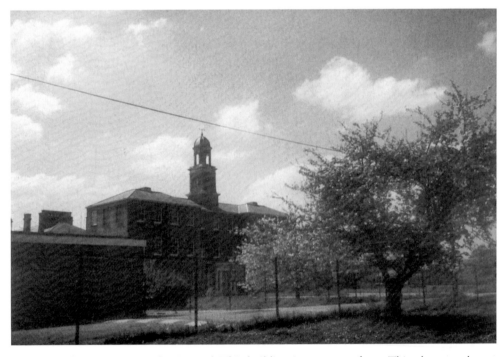

Ravenswood House at Knowle Hospital. This building is now out of use. This photograph was taken in 1998.

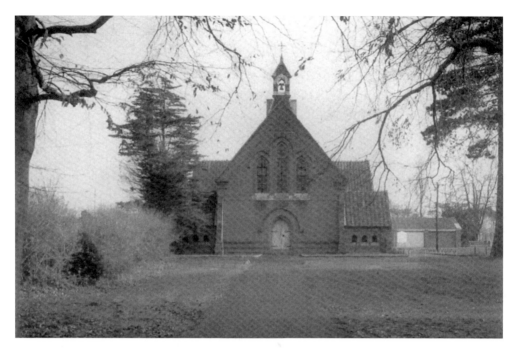

The old church at Knowle, near Ravenswood House.

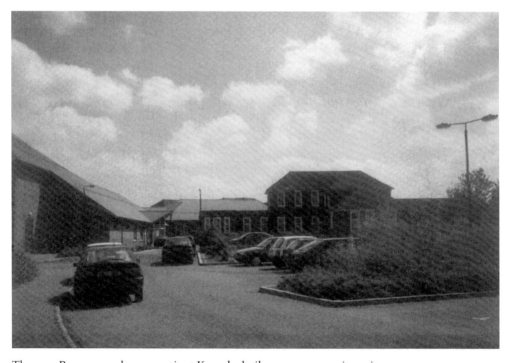

The new Ravenswood secure unit at Knowle, built on a new, spacious site.

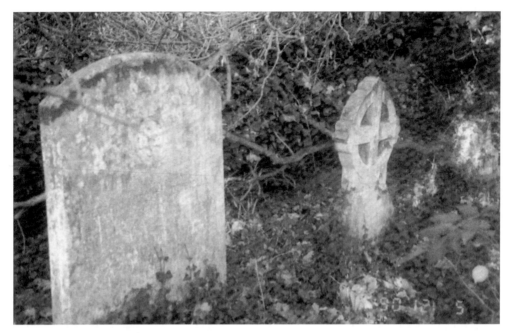

Near the new Ravenswood, but on the left of the road, is a sadly neglected little graveyard containing quite a few graves, some with headstones.

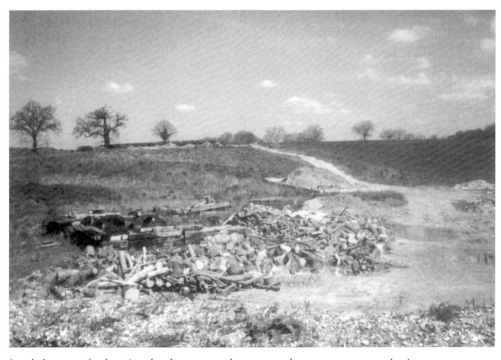

Land clearance for housing development and a new road across country to the A32.

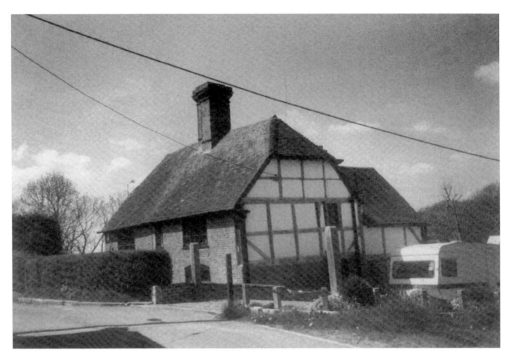

No. 4, Knowle Farm Cottages. Knowle Farm buildings have become the North Park Business Centre. This photograph was taken in 1998.

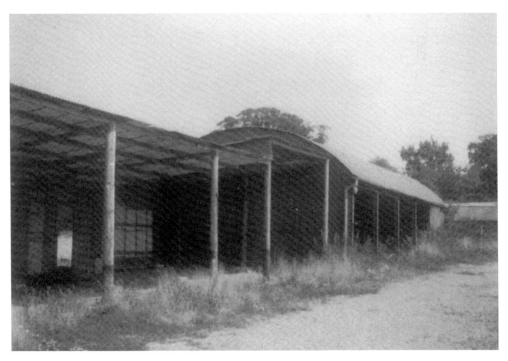

This, and the two following photographs, show Knowle Farm buildings in 1990.

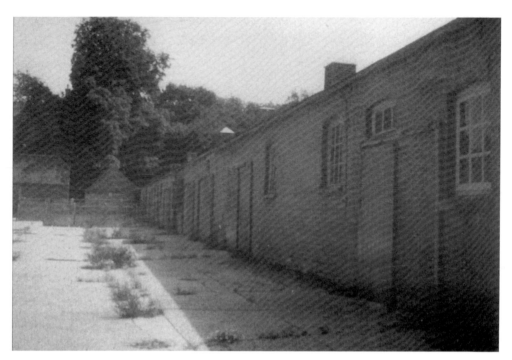

Farm buildings prior to restoration.

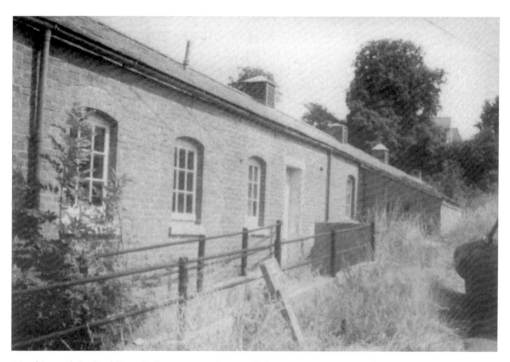

The front of the buildings before restoration work began.

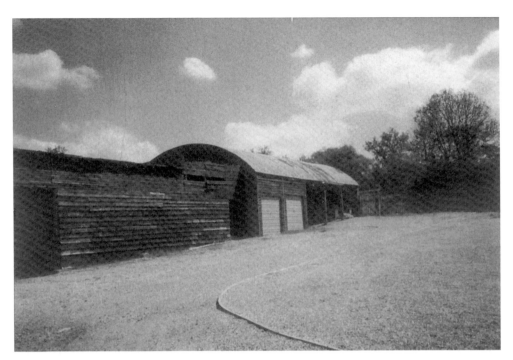

Renovated farm buildings.

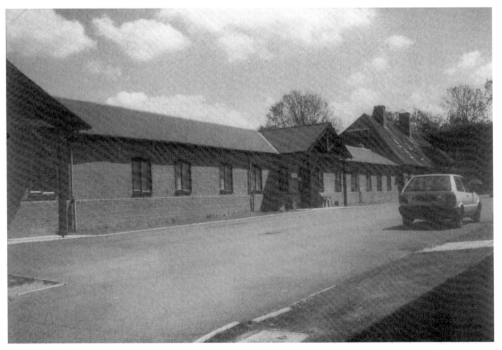

Restored and renovated buildings which are now the offices in the North Park Business Centre. Note the magnificent house at the end of the row.

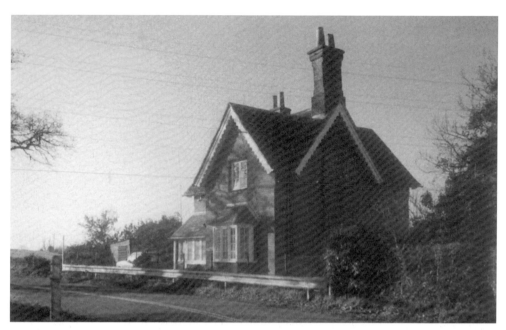

This house lies at the end of Knowle land, close to Wickham. The post on the left was used to put a chain across the road once a year, to indicate that the road is private. Now known as Mayles Lane, after the farm further along, it was, in less politically correct times, known as 'Lunatic Lane' – as can be seen on old postcards.

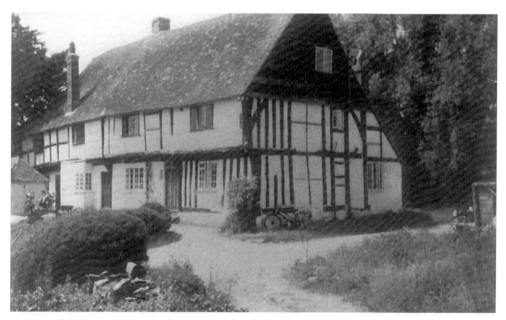

On the road between Wickham and Titchfield, we find Great Fontley Farm, which is dated at least to the fifteenth century and is said by some to be the oldest building of its type in the county. It is not, however, on the Borough Treasures List for the Fareham area.

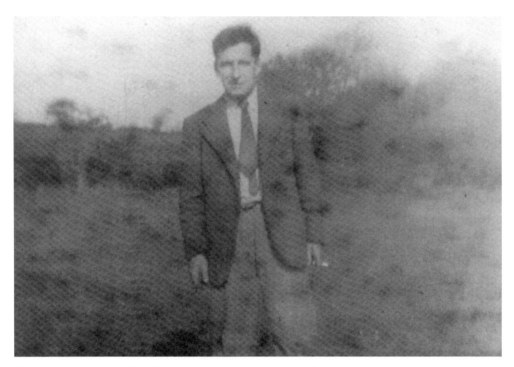

The late Commander H. L. Dickson, owner of the farm in the 1940s.

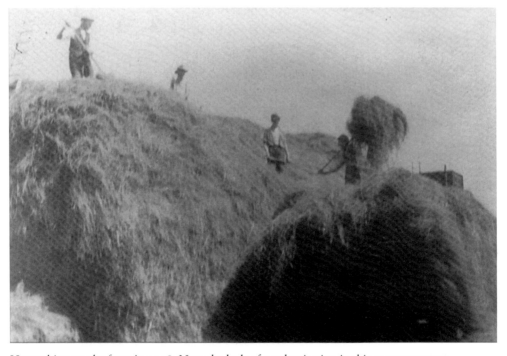

Haymaking on the farm in 1948. Note the lack of mechanisation in this post-war scene.

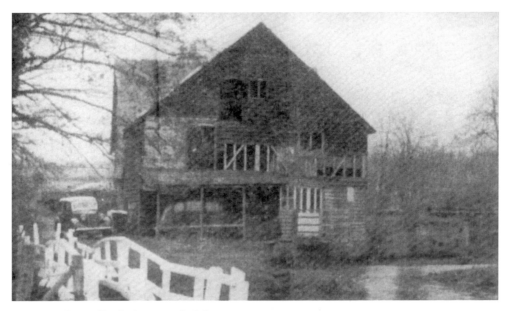

Great Fontley Mill, which was pulled down in 1948.

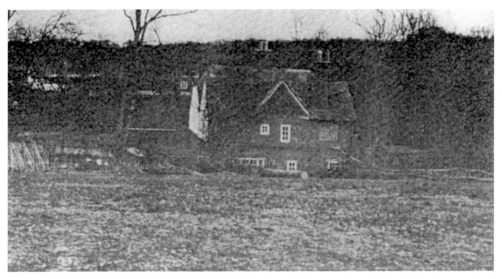

Continuing on towards Titchfield, Iron Mill Lane leads to the old Ironmaster's House. This is the last remaining part of Henry Cort's Great Fontley iron works. At one time, Samuel Jellicoe lived here. It is interesting to note that the road does a dogleg here: the map shows that this was probably a crossroads, as a footpath comes in from Fareham and another from Longwater Bridge.

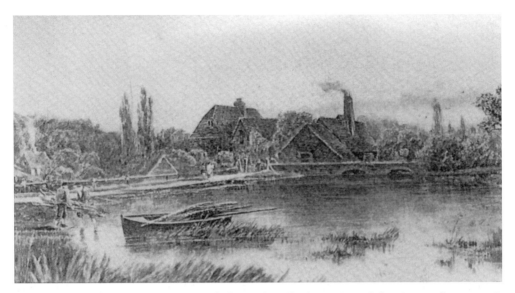

Fontley iron mills from a painting by Blatherwick in the latter part of the nineteenth century. It was here that Henry Cort was to revolutionise the iron industry (see page 52). The millpond has since dried up and everything here had disappeared until a 'dig' revealed the foundations.

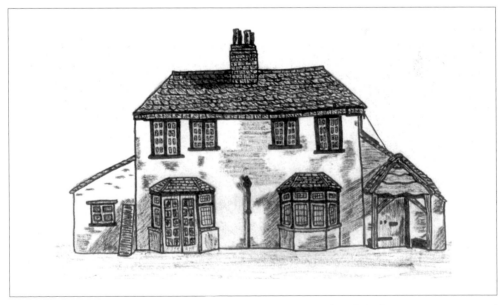

Iron Mill Cottages. Originally two cottages, this building was demolished in 1963. Once part of a set of four buildings, and used for the workers at the iron mills, they were mainly the homes of foresters and gamekeepers. Ships' timbers were used in these buildings and the cottages also had Sussex iron backs, dating from the reign of William and Mary.

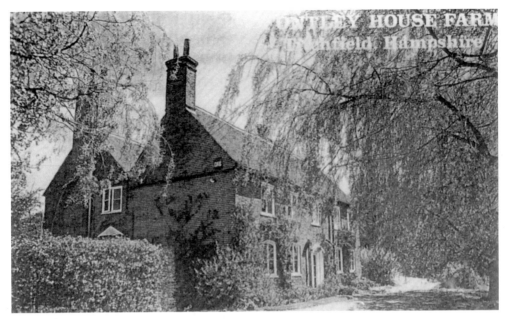

Fontley House Farm is also in this area and was last sold in 1986. Its fields have wonderful names such as 'Far East', 'Near East', 'Danzig', 'Pond Fork' and 'Grave' field.

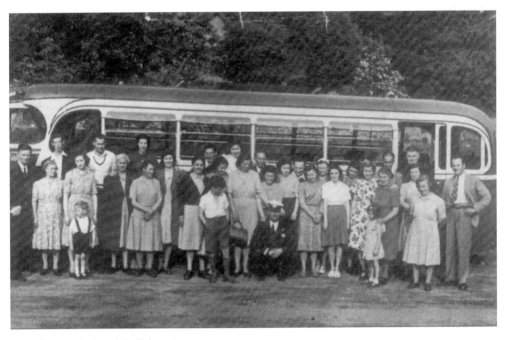

Knowle Hospital Social Club outing.

Four

Along the Wickham Road

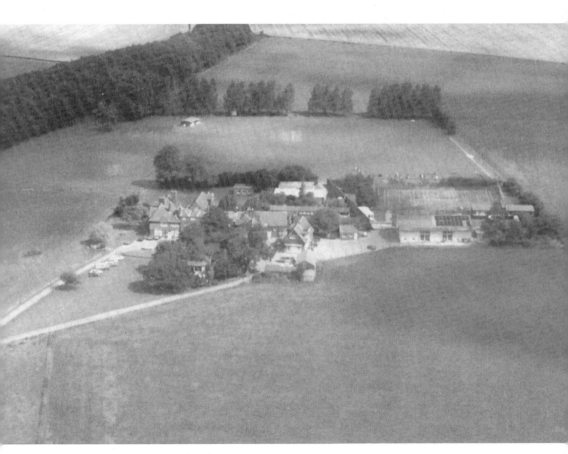

Aerial view of Boundary Oak School.

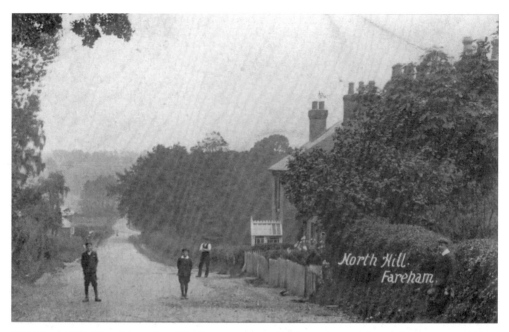

Old North Hill. The old road to Wickham came up Old Turnpike and down the very steep hill to link with the old Wickham Road, just before the M27 bridge.

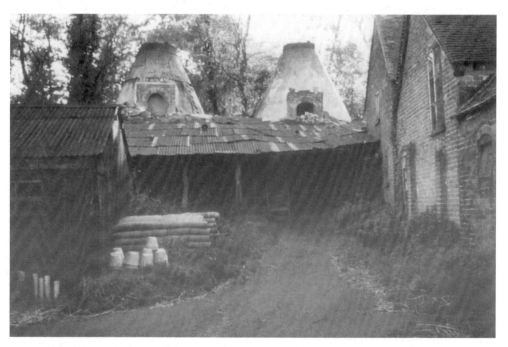

Here, until 1966, were the Fareham Potteries, owned by the Sandy family. Most of the pots were handmade. Bought out by Denmead Potteries, the potters were taken on but worked on fine pottery for the London market and abroad.

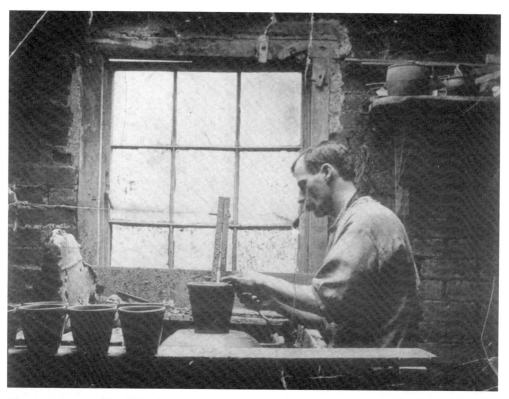

The master potter. The BBC television *Interlude* of the potter's wheel was based on his work.

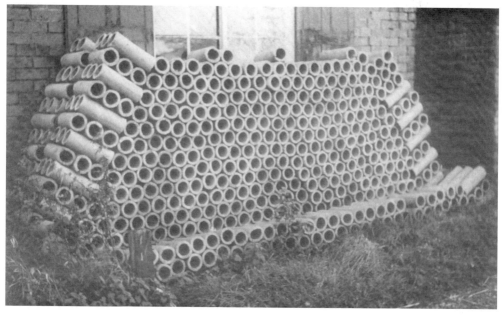

Drainage pipes stacked ready for sale.

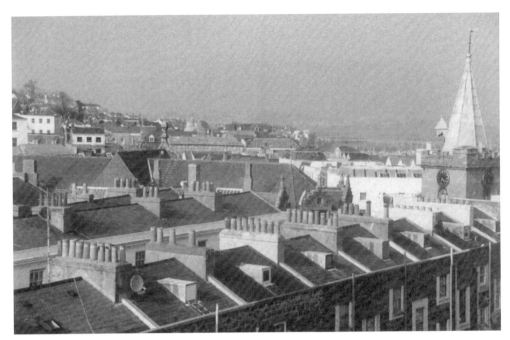

Fareham chimney pots in St Peter Port, Guernsey – proof that Fareham pots and tiles were extensively exported. There are at least seventy-eight in this picture!

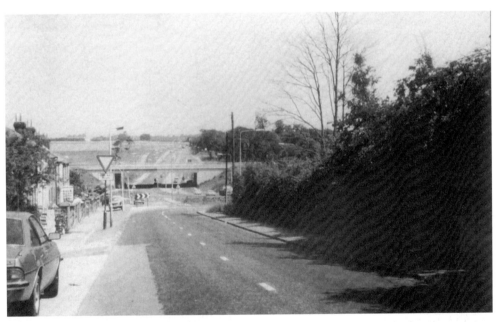

A foreshortened North Hill. There are potters' cottages on the left and, at this time (1980), there was yet another clay pit. The land is now built upon and it was necessary to drive piles in to support the houses. The distant woods on the right hide Boundary Oak School and the open farmland on the left provides a welcome break from urban sprawl.

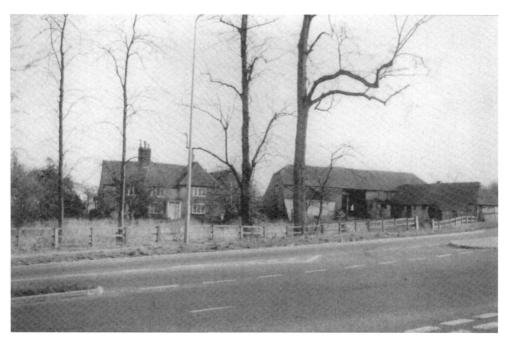

Furze Hill Farm in 1978. It stands at the junction of North Hill and the Wickham Road but is now the centre of a large office complex.

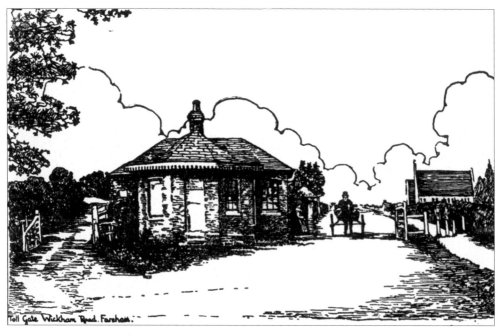

We return to the Turnpike Garage with a print showing the old tollhouse and the new tollgate on the new Turnpike Road, now known as the A32. It is interesting that many villagers up the Meon Valley still refer to 'going home along the turnpike'.

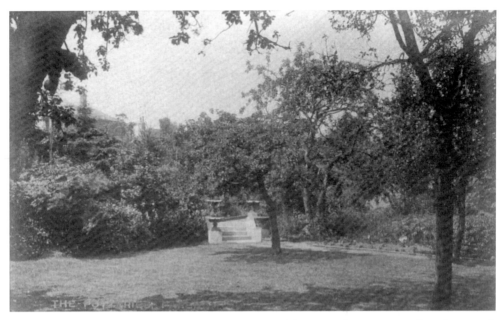

The Potteries – the late Mr Sandy's house on the Wickham Road. Five acres of garden stretch back to Old Turnpike and along the Wickham Road, landscaped from the old clay pit.

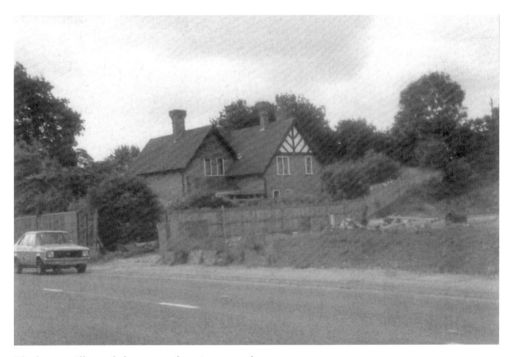

The house still stands but a new housing estate has grown.

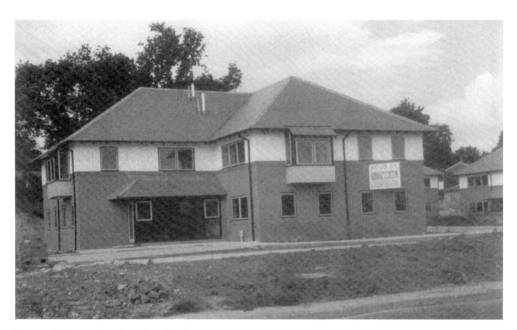

Some of the modern housing development.

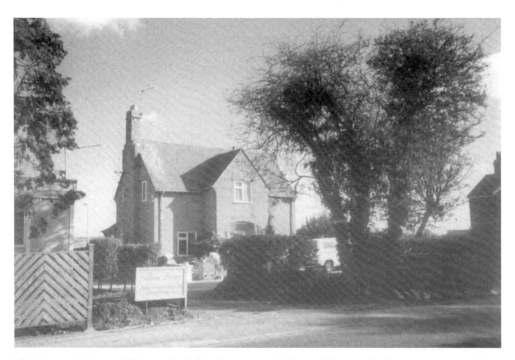

The Master's House. This was built for the master of the workhouse. The last master was Mr M. Worlock.

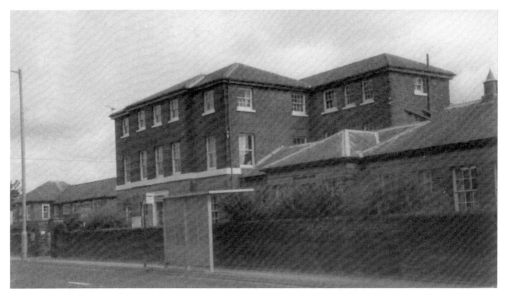

St Christopher's Hospital, now much enlarged, grew up in and around the old workhouse.

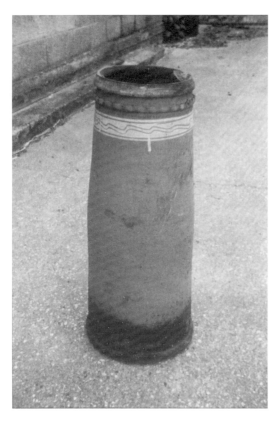

A Fareham Red chimney pot made at
Mr Harris's pottery on Fareham Common.
Note the 'pie crust' top.

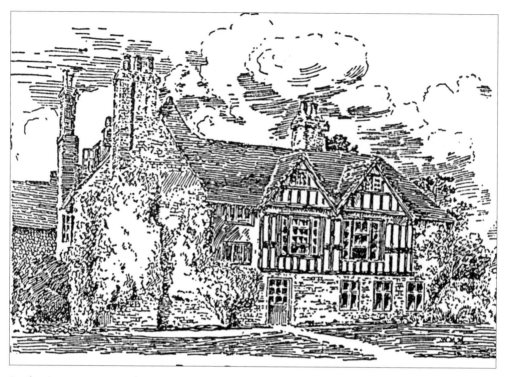

Roche Court, now Boundary Oak School, lies on the right of the road and has a joint entrance to modern Pook Lane. The original house was built by Peter des Roches in the thirteenth century.

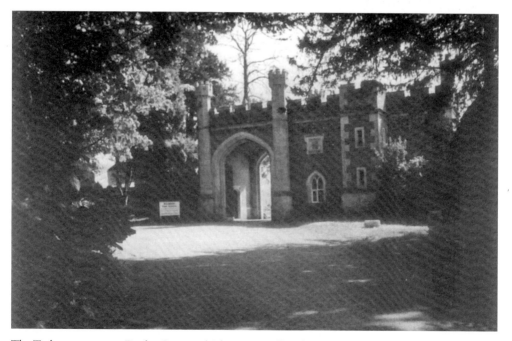

The Tudor gateway to Roche Court, which was castellated in 1808.

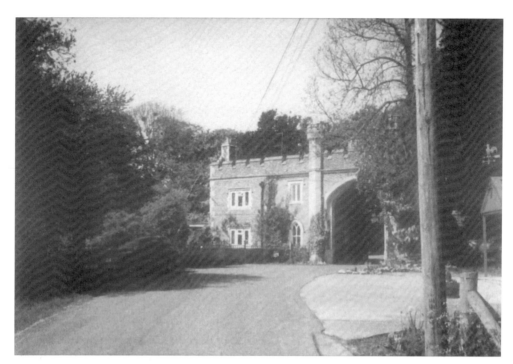

The Tudor gatehouse looking back.

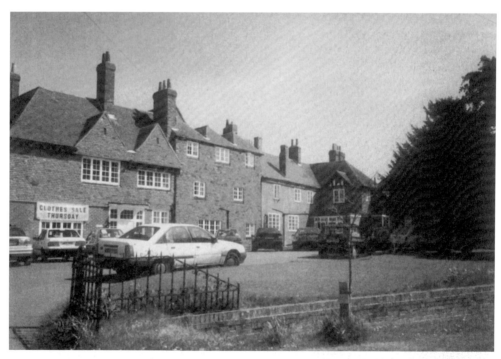

The front of the building with the hung Fontley Red handmade tiles.

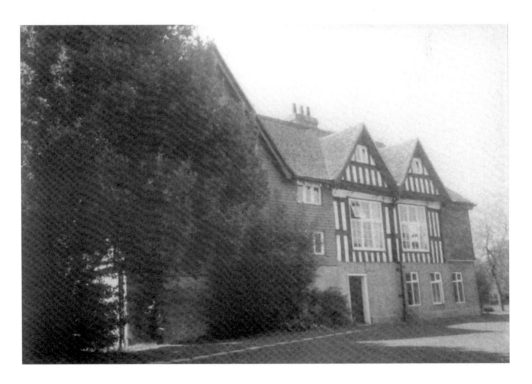

Right: Part of the medieval corridor with its stone floor, which probably dates back to the time of Peter des Roches, when it was a medieval hunting lodge. It was suggested that the floors be relaid, with modern tiles, but this was vehemently rejected by the headmaster as it is part of the original Roche Court, which is of great interest to historians.

Below: The back of the building shows the old outer wall and the original doorway. The artist, Fudge, did an excellent engraving of this.

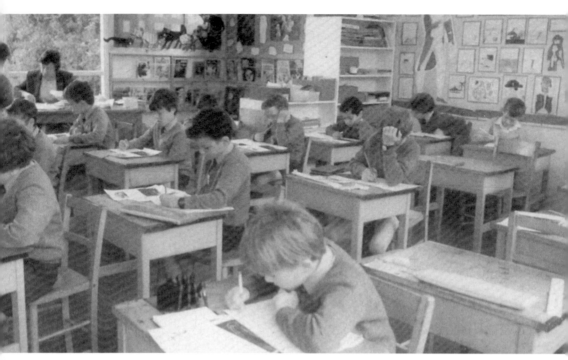

'School's in': how good to see everyone facing front where the blackboard is!

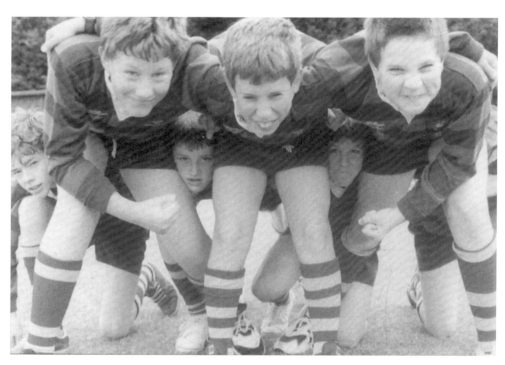

Does anyone recognise a son or brother?

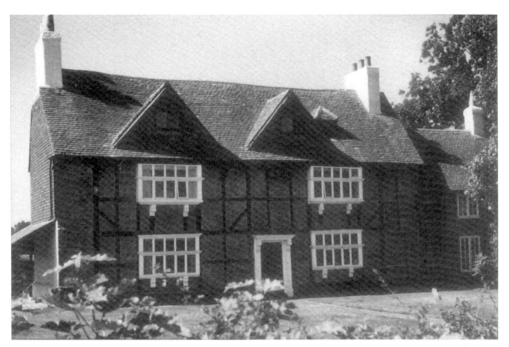

Dean farm is set back from the road and is a sixteenth-century, timber-framed building lying next to Hellyer's Farm and on the edge of old Fareham Common. The common is now mainly lost to housing.

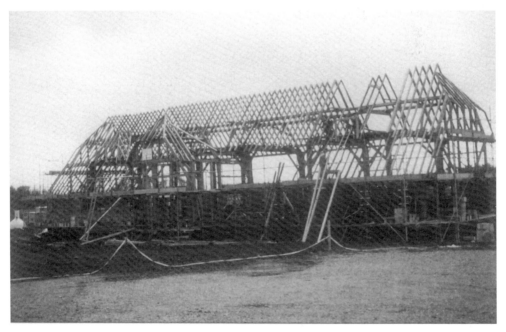

An old tithe barn found derelict near Bishops Waltham was moved to Dean Farm in 1989 to be restored.

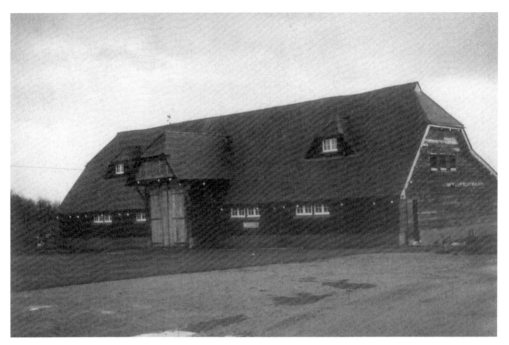

The completed barn in February 1990.

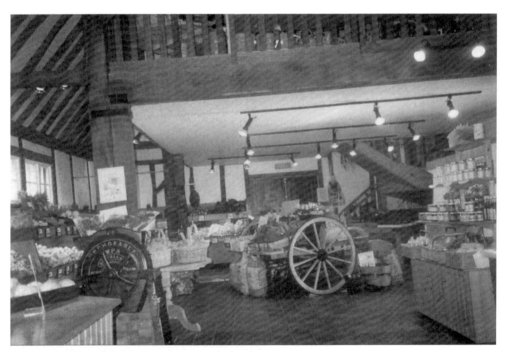

The interior of the shop in November 1990 – full of good things.

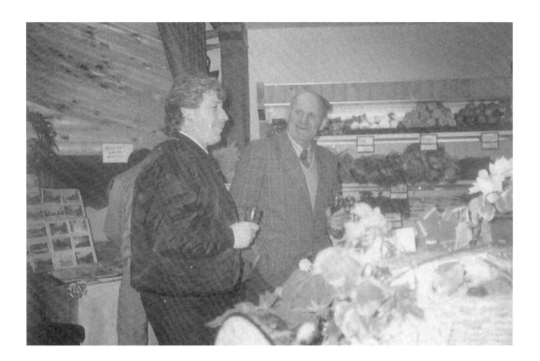

Above: A celebration, Christmas 1990. Facing the camera is Gerry Etherington, who had been at Dean Farm since he was a boy, celebrating over fifty years on the farm and living in the farmhouse.

Right: David Rees, the general manager who was responsible for the rescue of the old barn and the development of the farm shop, with the store's magnificent diversity of goods.

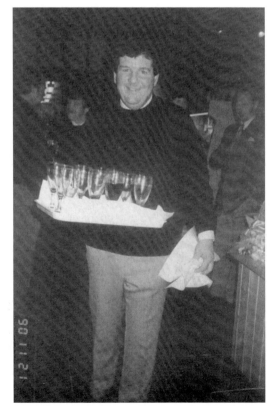

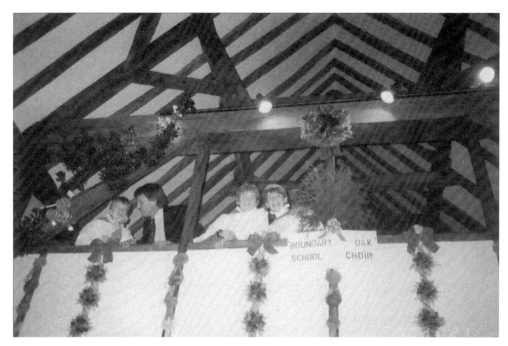

Christmas shopping evening and the choirboys from Boundary Oak School. Sadly, in spite of the fact that it was flourishing, the shop closed in 1995.

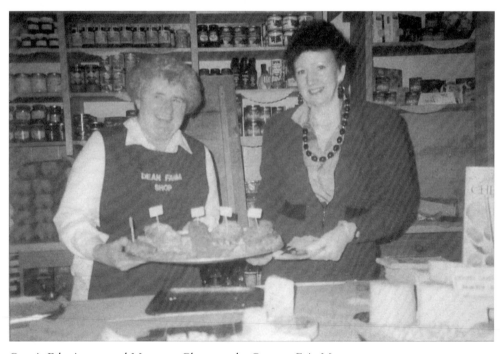

Connie Etherington and Margaret Glover at the Country Fair, May 1993.

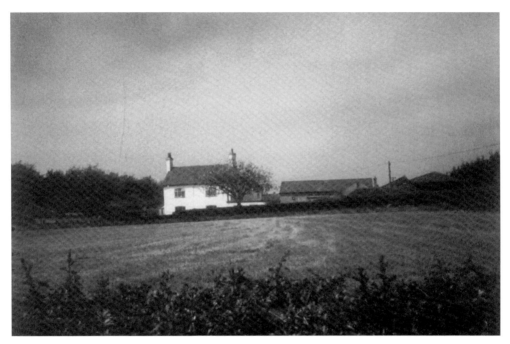

Albany Farm, which was once called Pear Tree Farm, on the right-hand side of the road.

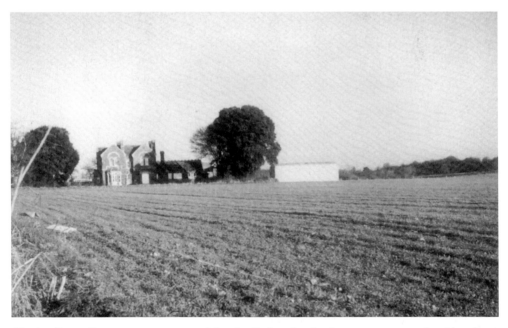

Charity Farm. For many years owned by the Parker family, it was once owned, with a large amount of land, by William Price. Funds from the land helped to found Price's School and Price's Charity.

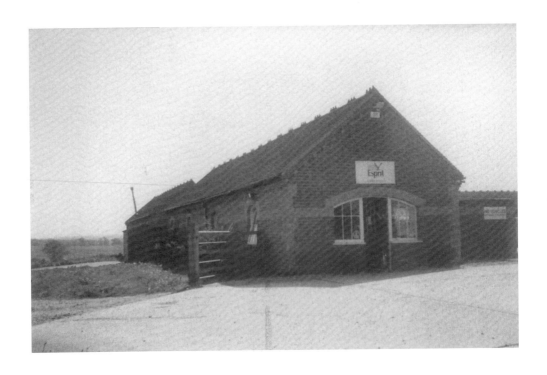

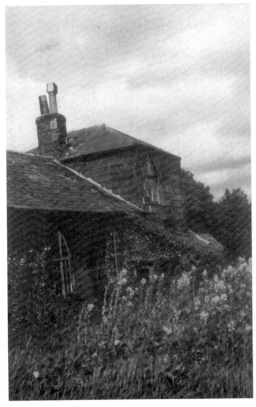

Above: Albany Farm buildings, now used for light industry and offices. Near here, a road from Knowle now joins the A32.

Left: Crocker Hill church, which for many years served the local community. It lay on Forest Road.

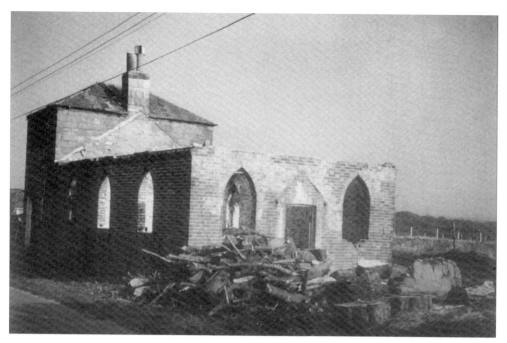

The church was sold and demolished in 1981.

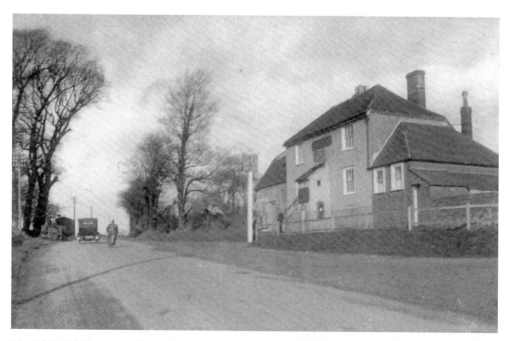

The 'old' Old Vine, a building that went back to the days of George III. It stood to the left of the present building.

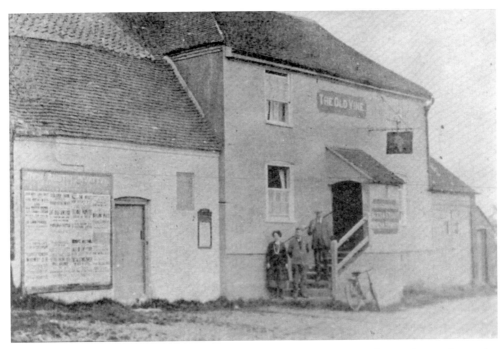

Another view of the 'old' Old Vine which, in 1924, was the scene of a triple murder and a suicide. The pub was full that evening.

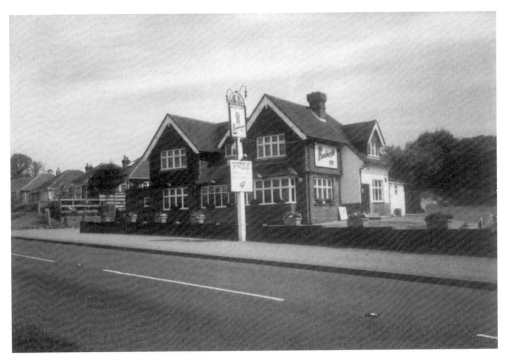

The 'new' Old Vine, renamed 'Banbury's'.

Five

East of Fareham

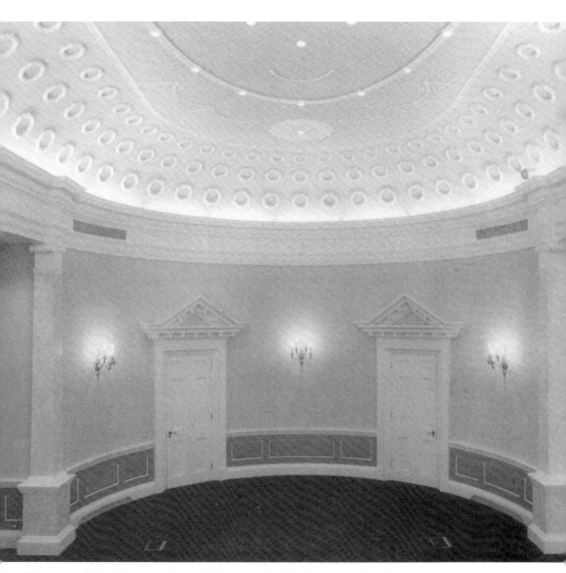

The restored Oval Room at Cams Hall now reached by the restored staircase.

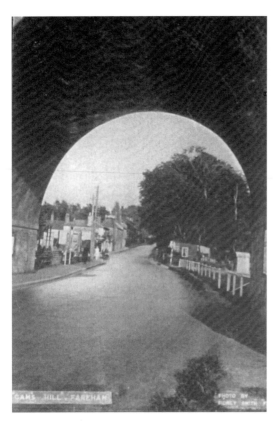

Left: Old Cams Hill, the Delmé Arms and the site of the old mill, on the right.

Below: To get your bearings, the Delmé Arms stands at the foot of old Cams Hill. It was previously known as the Horse and Groom.

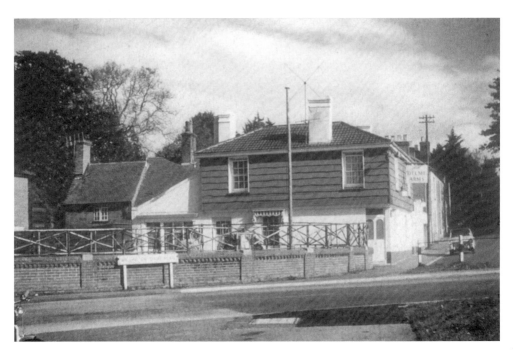

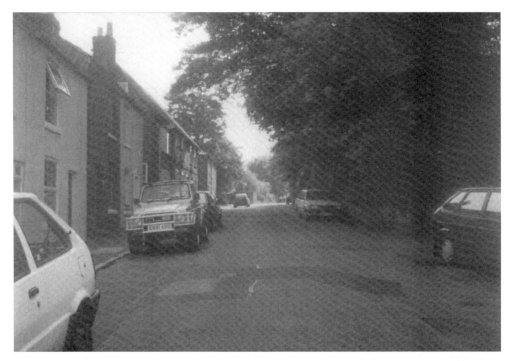

The present Cams Hill, now very 'gentrified'.

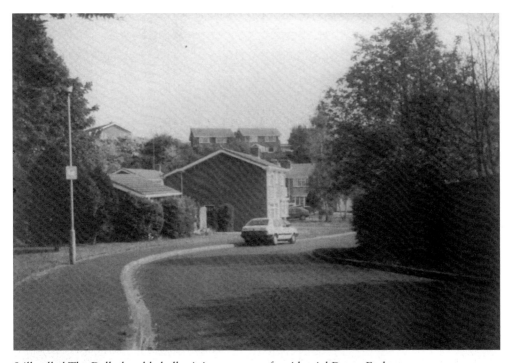

Still called The Dell, the old chalk pit is now part of residential Down End.

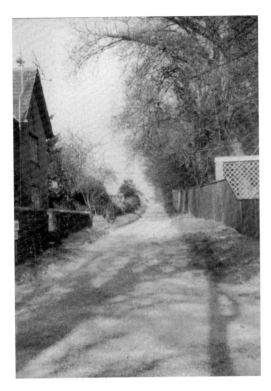

Old Paradise Lane, a long-time right of way.

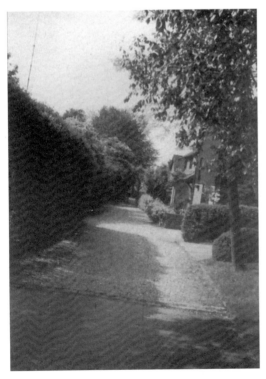

Paradise Lane in 1998, now swamped by housing. The high hedges mark where the old stables used to be.

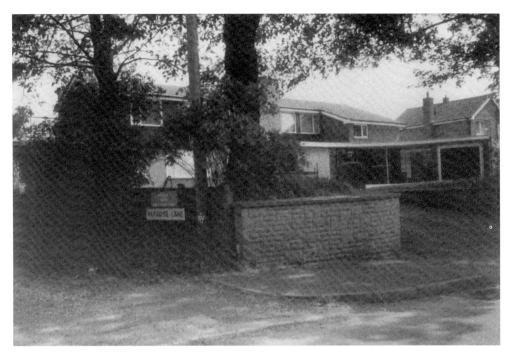

More modern development off Paradise Lane.

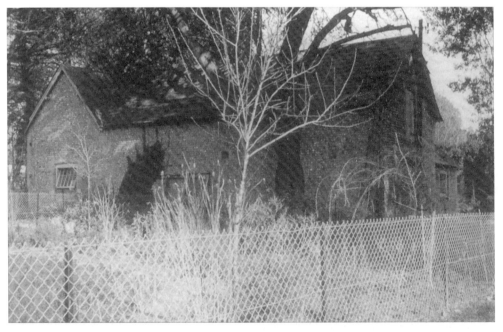

The Down End House stables: now destroyed to make way for housing.

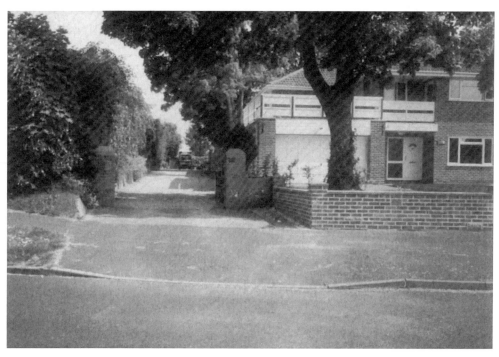

A house blocks the right of way here – although straight through the garden might be an idea!

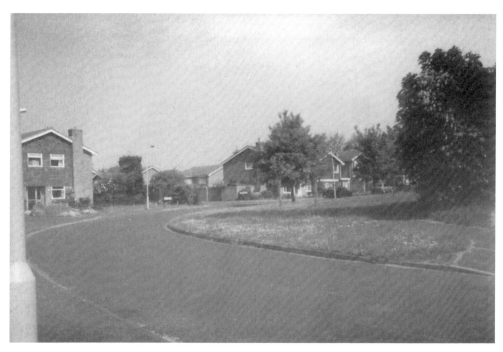

The diversion for the right of way is through about a quarter of a mile of houses. There appears to be no notice telling of this diversion.

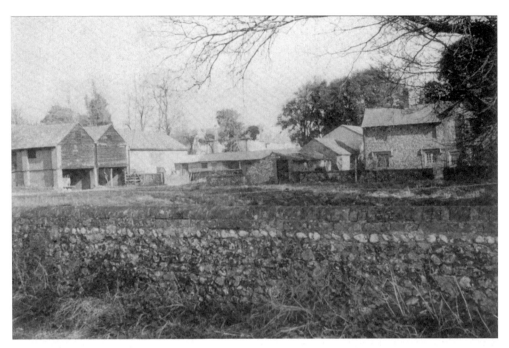

Old Down End Farm and buildings. Note the dressed flint work.

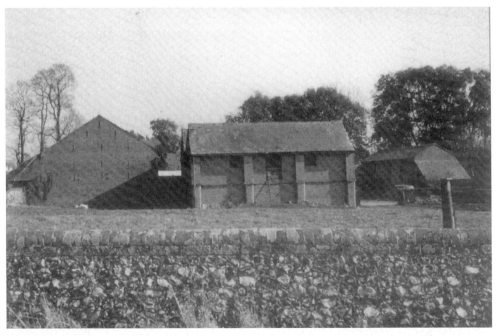

Down End Farm with its brick, double-roofed barn and dovecot. It is now difficult to find any farm buildings in this area and certainly much of the capped flint wall has disappeared.

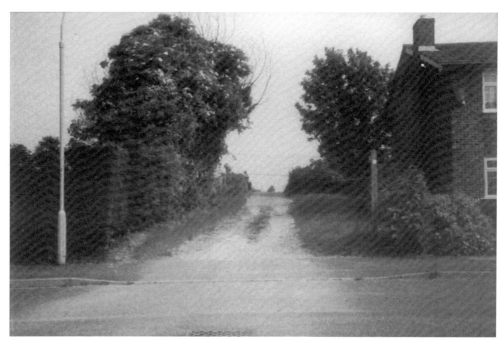

Paradise Lane regained! This leads to the bridge over the railway and, on the right, one would be passing Down End Farm.

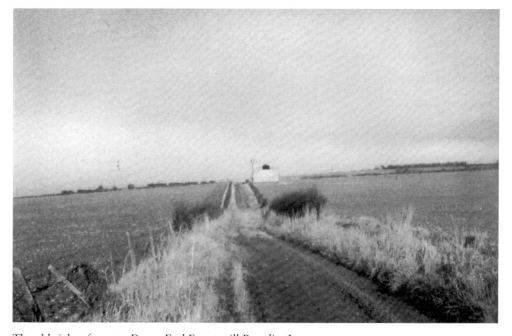

The old right of way to Down End Farm, still Paradise Lane.

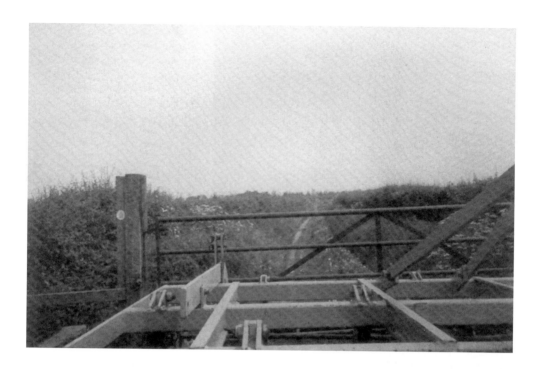

Above: Just beyond the railway bridge, the same view of the footpath, now nearly lost because of lack of use and machinery placed in the way of the casual walker (there is a stile).

Right: The newly restored staircase at Cams Hall. Much of the original stone and some of the iron was used.

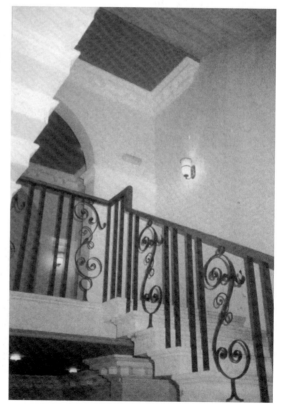

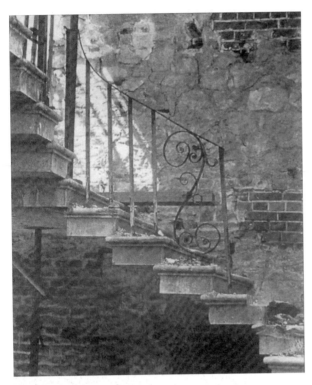

Left: The original staircase at Cams Hall was described as 'The Admirably Constructed Stone Staircase. Of good width and most easy ascent with wrought iron balustrades, leads to the Principal Landings on the First Floor'. The restored staircase leads to the Oval Room (see page 85).

Below: A beautifully constructed fireplace in the restored Oval Room.

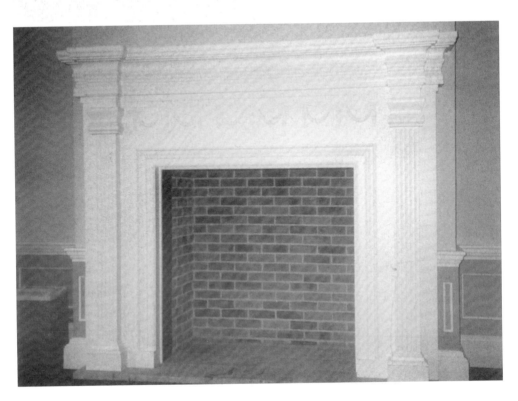

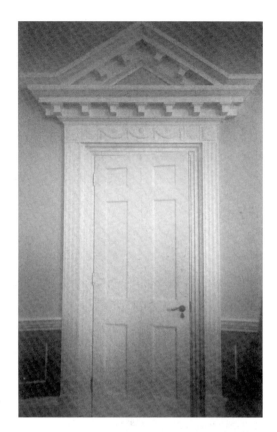

Right: A reconstructed door in the Oval Room.

Below: Taken in 1994, this shows the ruined dovecot and the end of the barn.

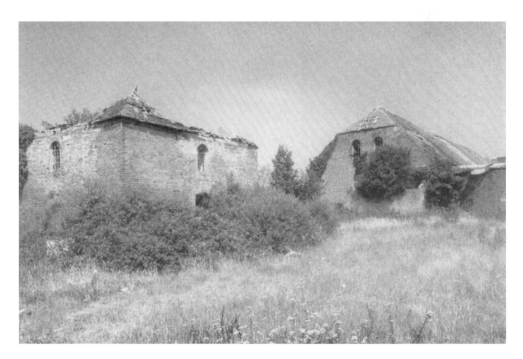

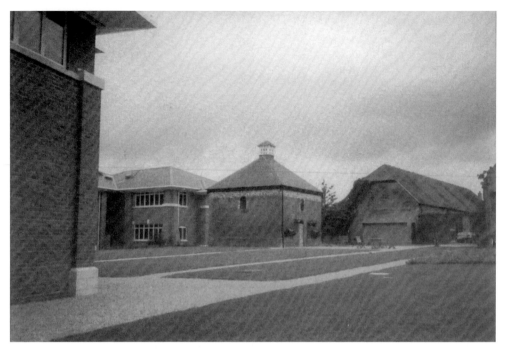

The same view in 1998, with the addition of Delmé Place.

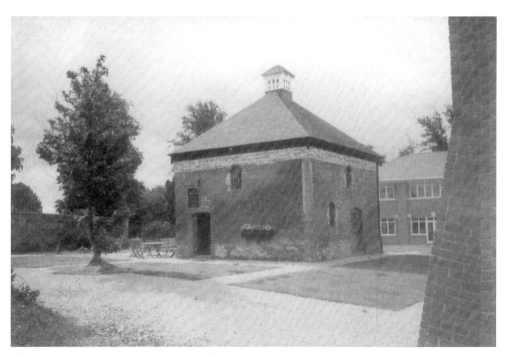

The restored Dovecot – now a snack and wine bar.

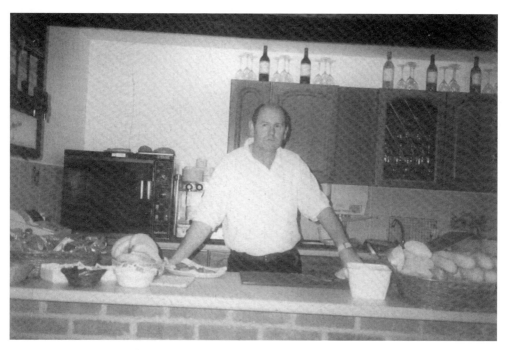

Mr G. Knipe, manager of the Dovecot, June 1998.

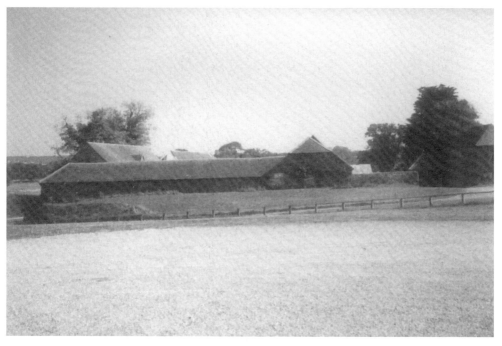

Boarhunt. The great tithe barn at Manor Farm, Boarhunt, 1998.

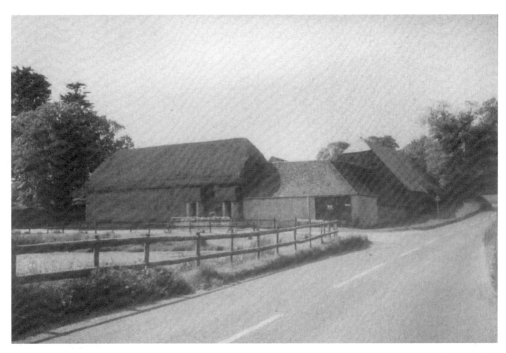

Round the corner to find the rest of the building of Manor Farm. The farmhouse itself lies in the trees on the left.

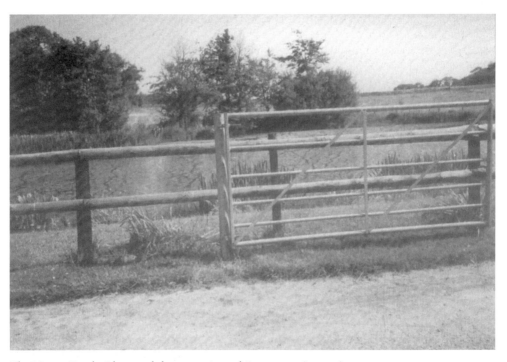

The Manor Pond – 'deep and dangerous' proclaims a warning notice.

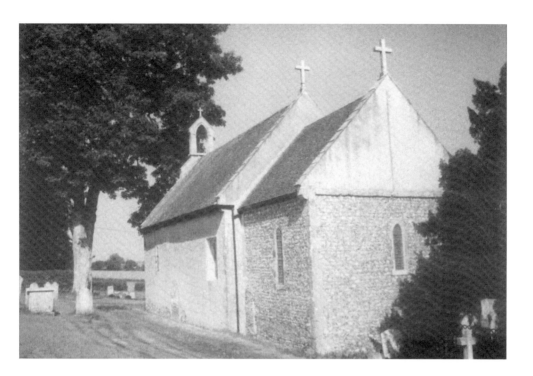

Above: St Nicholas church stands nearby on rising land. It is a Saxon church with a nineteenth-century roof. The Great Yew Tree is over 1,000 years old and the oldest in the county, with a circumference of twenty-seven feet. Local legend says that, in medieval times, a family sheltered within its hollowed trunk throughout an entire winter.

Right: Looking to the east end and, in the interior, the magnificent Saxon arch can be seen. The window at the east end is also old and built of chalk. The external window is of Bath stone, the glass is modern.

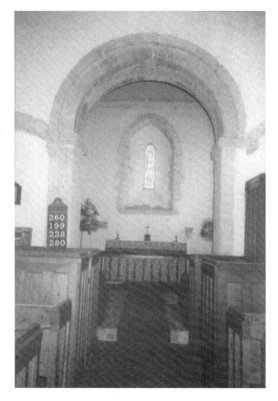

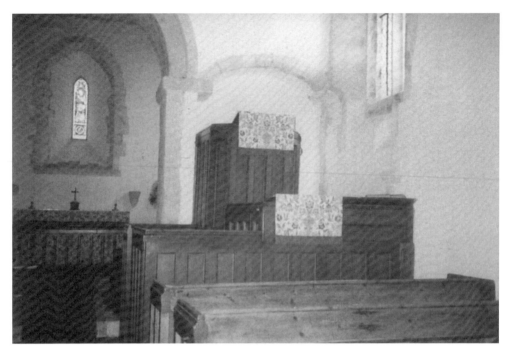

The three-decker pulpit dates from the restoration in 1853.

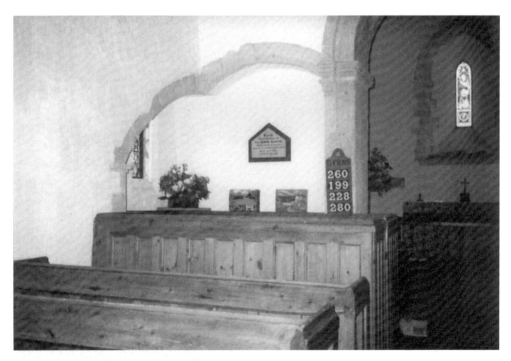

Opposite to the pulpit is the squire's box pew, which is still in use.

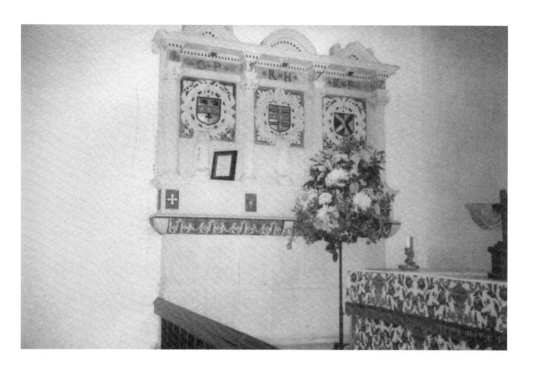

Above: This important Elizabethan monument to the Henslow family actually cost £5 when made by an itinerant Flemish mason. The Henslows were a prominent Roman Catholic family and known as 'persistent recusants' by the government of the time. Mrs Catherine Henslow was pressed for her fines from not attending church and she offered a 'protest before God' that she had only £20 to support herself and her servants, and offered the Queen twenty shillings, 'as poor widow's mite', to be allowed to practise her religion. There is a tablet to Thomas Henslow stating (in Latin): 'He fought the good fight, he finished his course, and he kept the faith'.

Right: Nelson's Monument on Portsdown Hill. It was put up within three years of the Battle of Trafalgar. Officers and men gave two days' pay 'to the memory of Lord Viscount Nelson ... to perpetuate his triumph and their regret'.

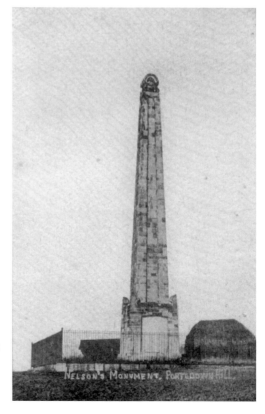

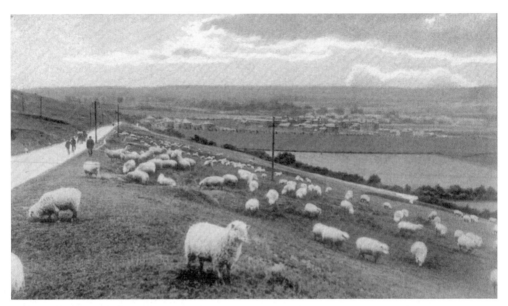

Open land on Portsdown Hill with arable land on the lower slopes. It was to remain like this until after the Second World War.

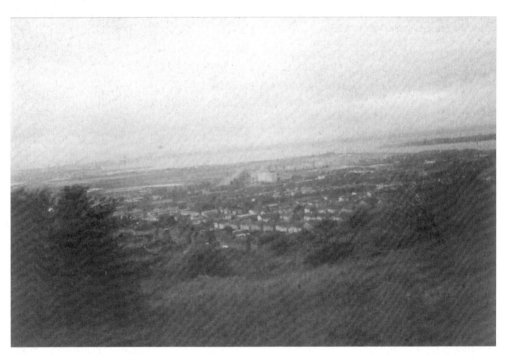

Overlooking Portsmouth and towards the Portchester peninsula in 1998. In the late nineteenth century, Cobbett commented on it, saying 'Eight miles of cornfields, here the first sheaf is cut in England'. Now there is scrub on the higher ground, housing on the middle ground and industry on the lower.

Six

Portchester

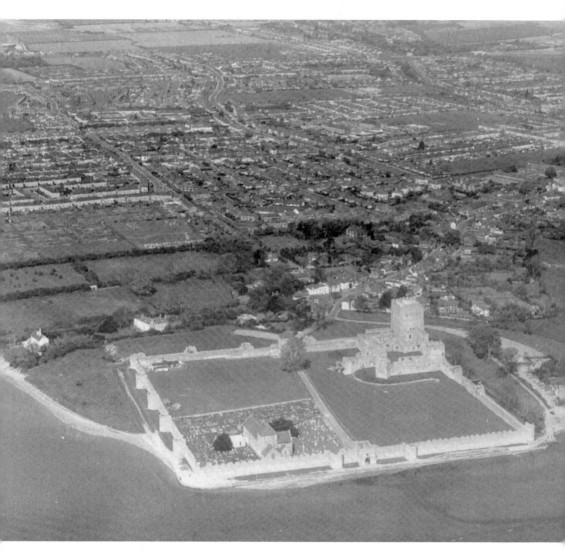

The castle from the air, clearly showing Roman walls, the church, the keep, and a large amount of open space. Castle Street is also in view.

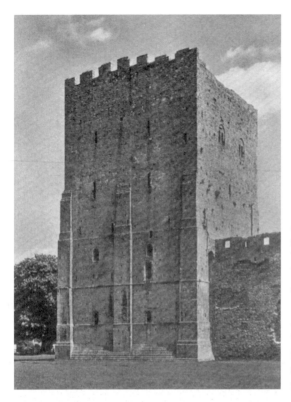

Left: The massive keep presides over a large area of open space, which has become a playground for Portchester, being used for festivals, pageants and cricket, to name a few pursuits.

Below: A 'dig' at the castle. Barry Cunliffe revealed the original Roman ground level and old foundations. The new gateway proved to point directly towards Roman Way.

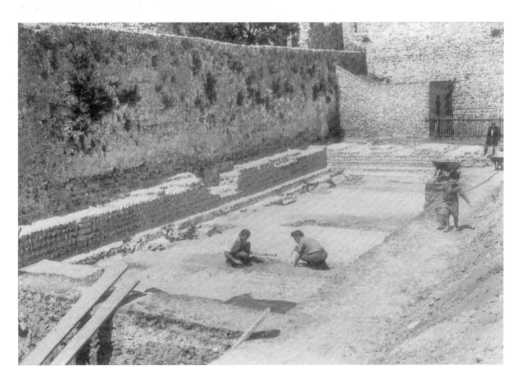

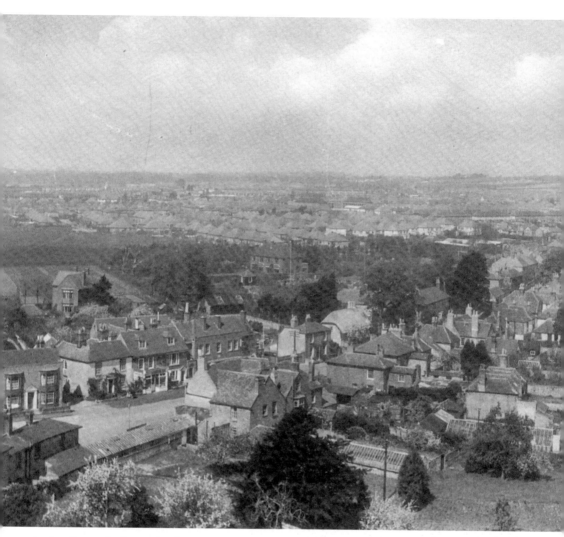

A view from the keep. Castle Street is clearly seen here, as is the urban sprawl. To the left is Roman Way which leads through to Wicor Mill and the Wicor bone works (now both gone) and linked up with the Lady Bridge in Fareham (now under the Delmé roundabout) and up Lysses Path towards, eventually, SS Peter and Paul church.

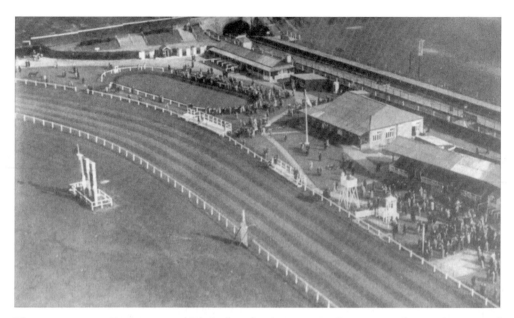

The racecourse at Paulsgrove, which had earlier been on Farlington marshes. It disappeared before the Second World War but was remembered by the bus conductors – 'Harbour Lights, Racecourse, Bert's Caff .... '!

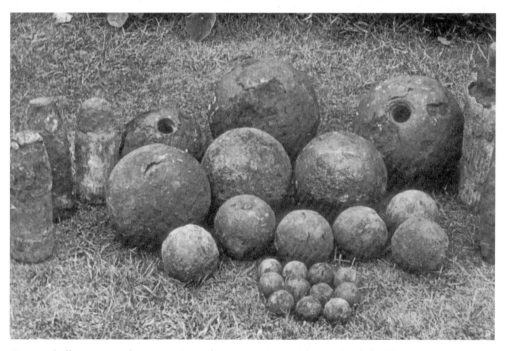

Cannon balls, once in the possession of Commander Cobham who led a Sea Scout group and organised searches when the weather and very low tides coincided.

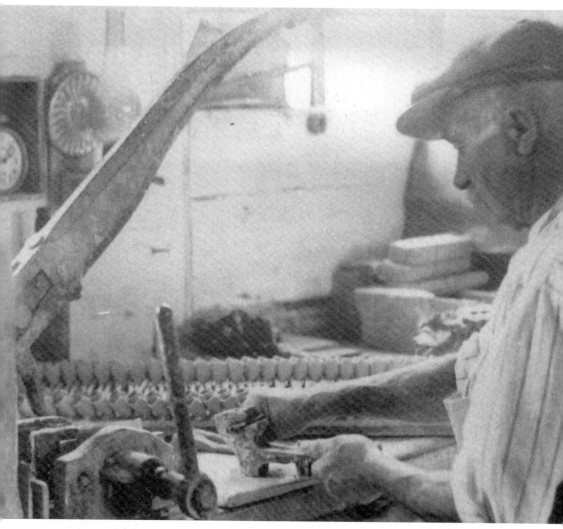

A magnificent photograph of Mr Baker, the pipe maker at Leigh's Pipe Works. The picture was taken in 1932 and shows the rows of completed pipes. The works closed in 1940, having lasted exactly 100 years.

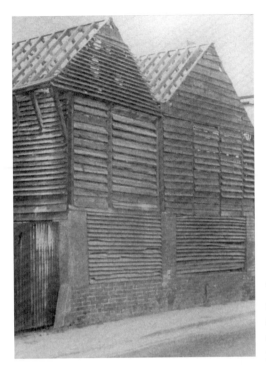

The old building of the clay pipe works; the roofs have been removed. The works stood at the end of Castle Street; a development company bought the building and land. This photograph was taken in 1968.

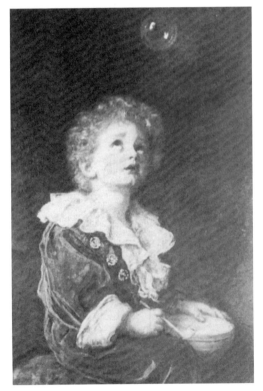

'Bubbles' by Millais. The boy grew up to be Admiral James: as a child, he lived in Turret House. He never lost his nickname.

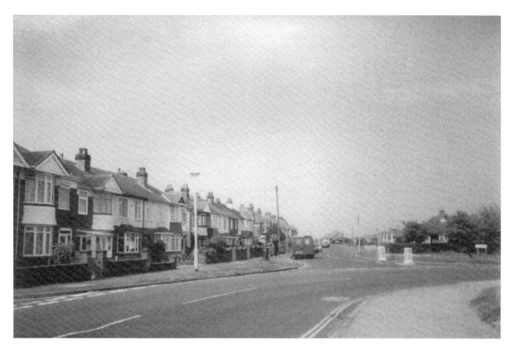

Cranleigh Road leading towards the site of the Wicor bone works. Housing has encroached on the area.

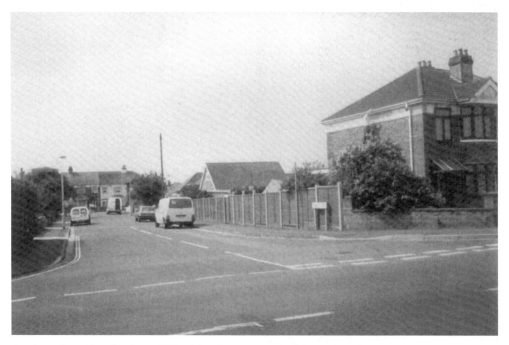

Sandport Road leading from White Hart Lane to much older property.

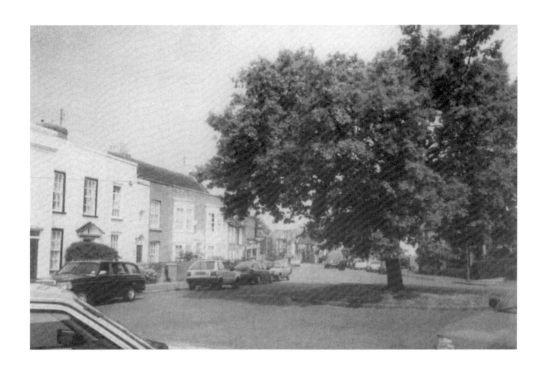

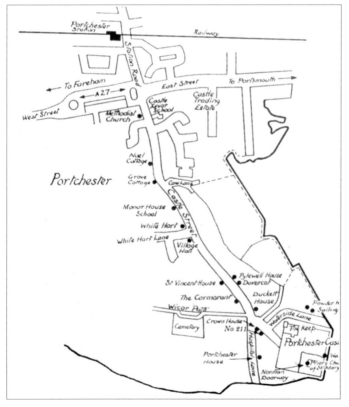

Above: Castle Street, taken from the Jubilee Oak, which was planted in 1935. The tree lies near the end of Castle Street on what was once the village square.

Left: A map of old Portchester showing the conservation area. The Portchester Society produced this.

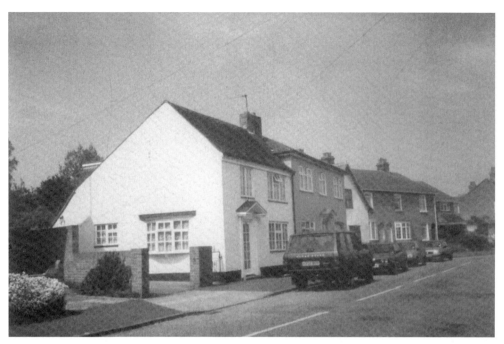

Portchester has lost its dairy, animal pound, smithy and clay-pipe factory, but still has some magnificent houses, of which these are a few.

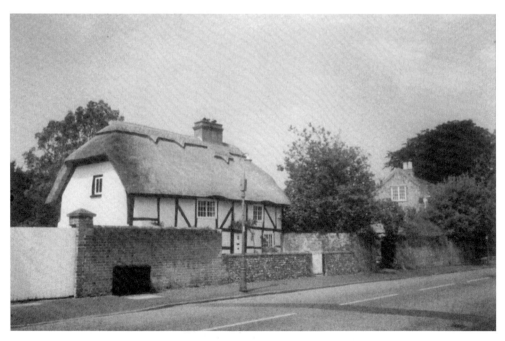

Thatched cottage, believed to be fifteenth century.

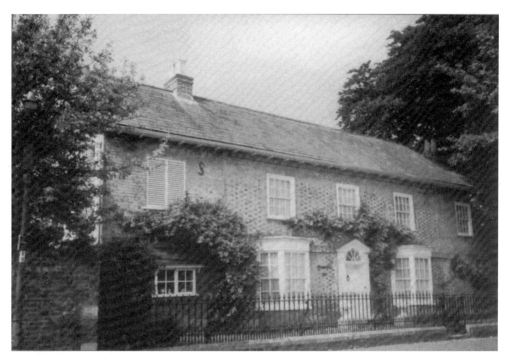

St Vincent House, named by Lord Nelson's Captain Cook after the battle of St Vincent.

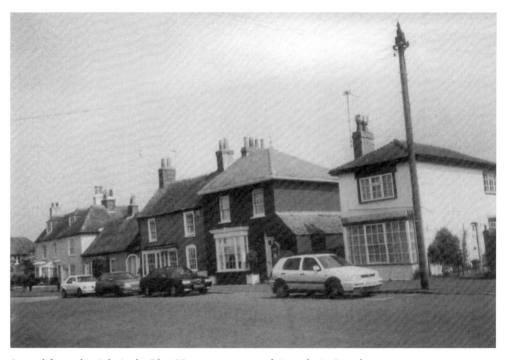

Second from the right is the Blue House, once one of six pubs in Portchester.

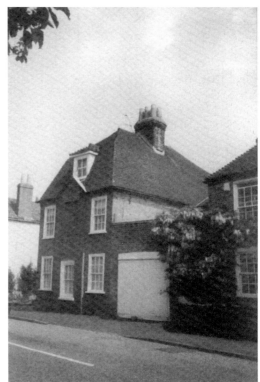

Right: 'Dovercot', dated 1702 with Georgian red bricks. This building was probably once a granary.

Below: The only surviving pub in this part of Castle Street – The Cormorant.

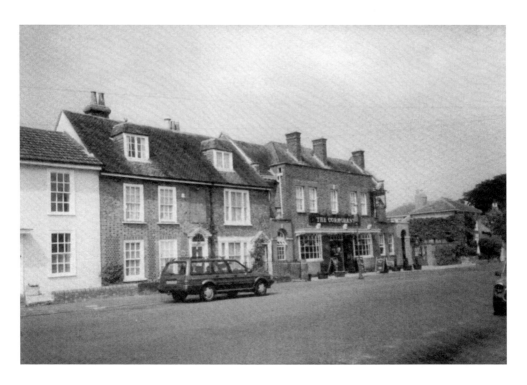

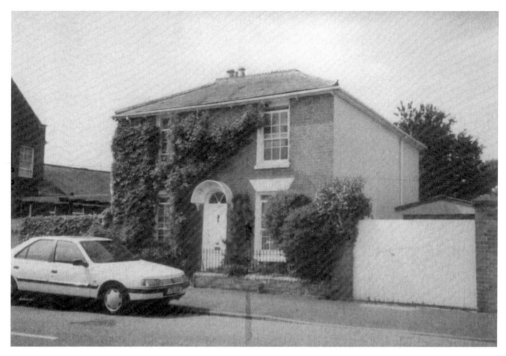

This, and the following three photographs, show some of the fine houses in Castle Street.

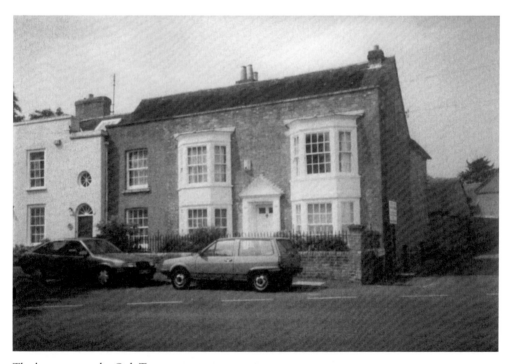

The houses near the Oak Tree.

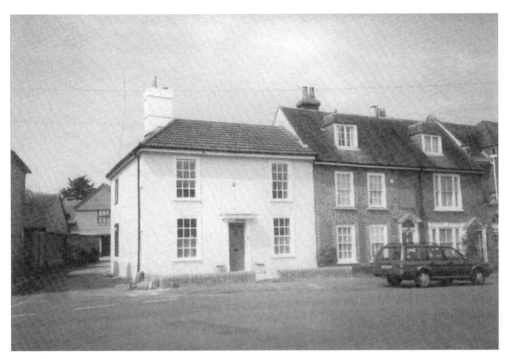

These two houses follow immediately alongside the previous pair, continuing north up Castle Street.

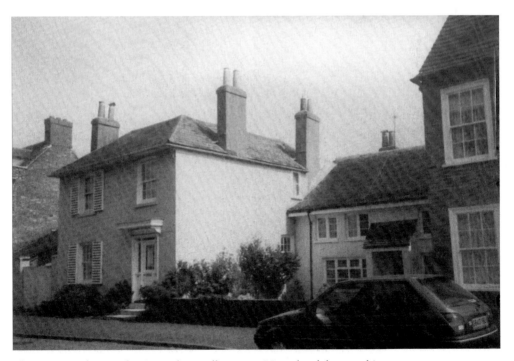

The Georgian houses dominate the small cottage. Note the elaborate chimneys.

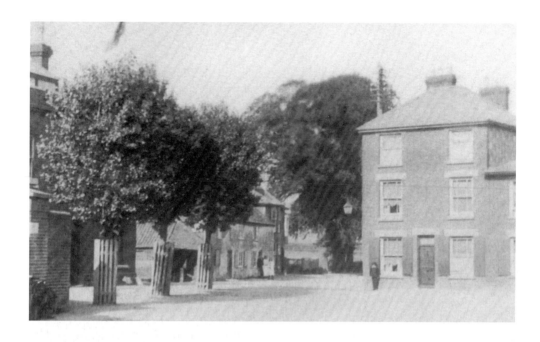

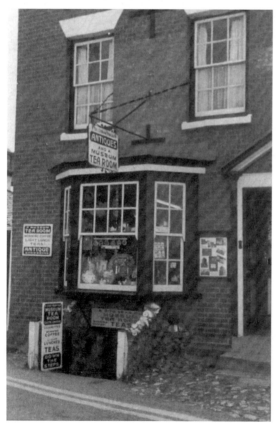

Above: An old view of the end of Castle Street, approaching the castle.

Left: The large house in the previous picture became an antique shop, while down below there was a tearoom. This was the museum's tearoom, which was going strong for many years after the Second World War.

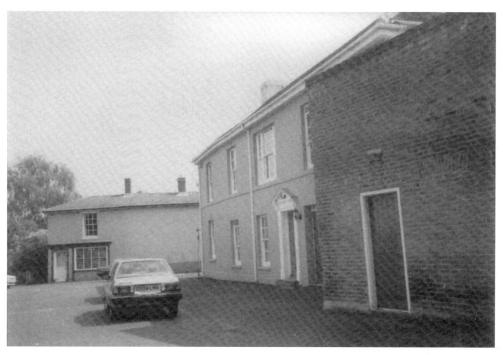

A picture taken in 1998 showing the same area. The delightful shop has disappeared.

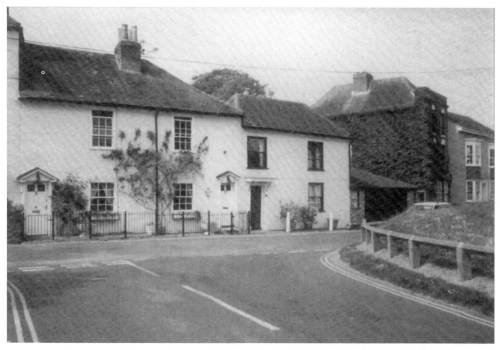

Houses lying opposite the road leading to the castle's car park.

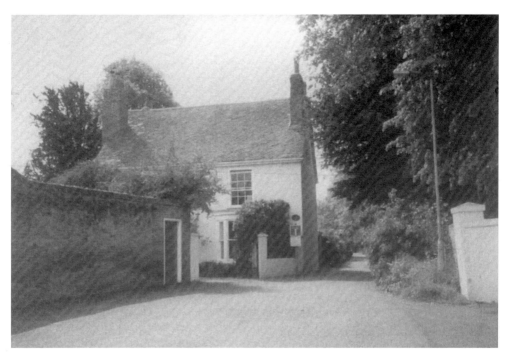

Hospital Lane leading to Portchester House. The lane branches off to the right of Castle Street.

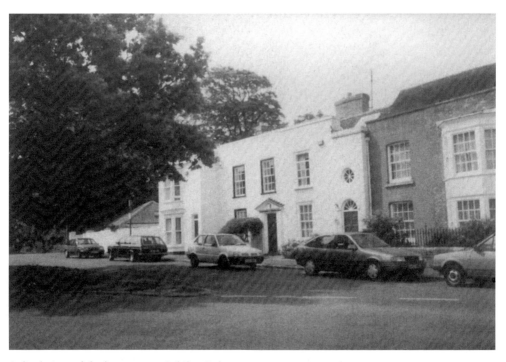

A final view of the houses near Jubilee Oak.

Seven

'Snippets'

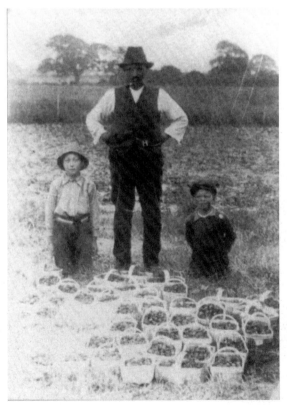

Strawberries at Titchfield. This photograph was from Mr T. Cox.

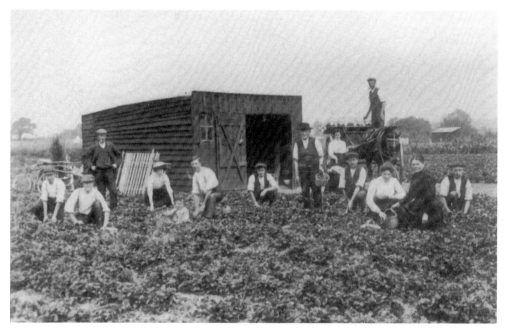

Strawberry pickers at Brook Lane, Warsash.

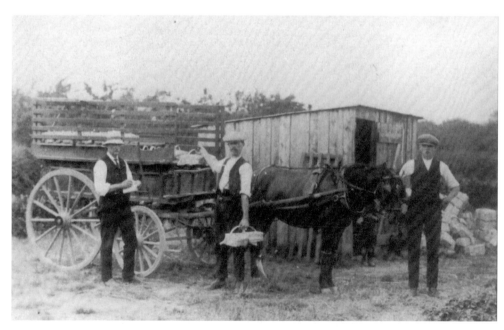

A typical Hampshire strawberry wagon with high sides to support the baskets. This photograph was also taken at Brook Lane, Warsash.

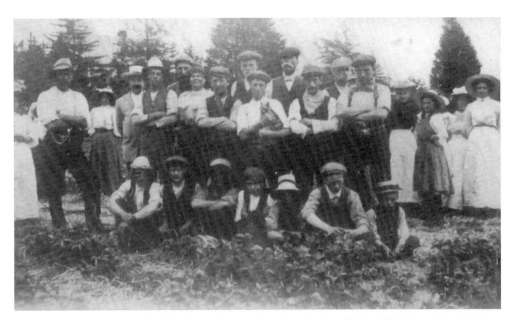

Strawberry pickers at Titchfield. The land was owned by Mr Jewell. Mrs Wield, a girl at the time, is third from the right. Don't forget the cat!

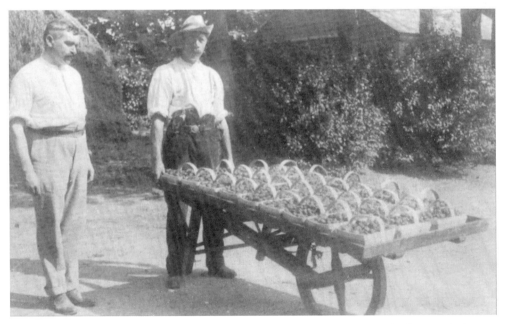

Mr Jewell on the left with his foreman. The strawberry cart is loaded with baskets – which were made in Swanwick.

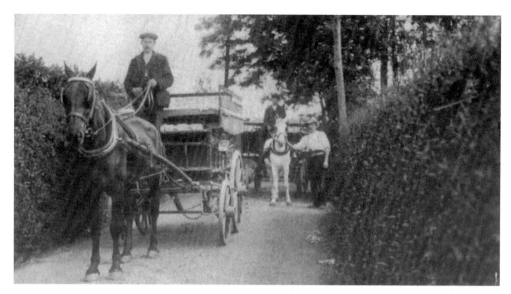

Stacked strawberry baskets on wagons about to go to Swanwick station, bound for Fareham and, later, London. Mr F. Wield is driving the wagon.

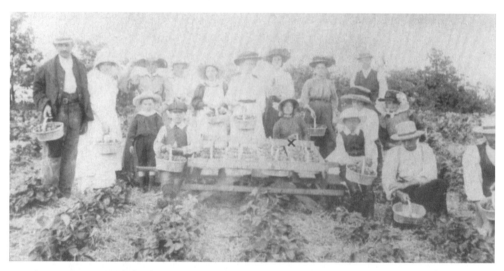

Local strawberry fields – the exact location is not known. Mrs Cooper's grandmother was Florence Elliot and here is Florence as a child, marked with an 'X'. Note the very large strawberry baskets.

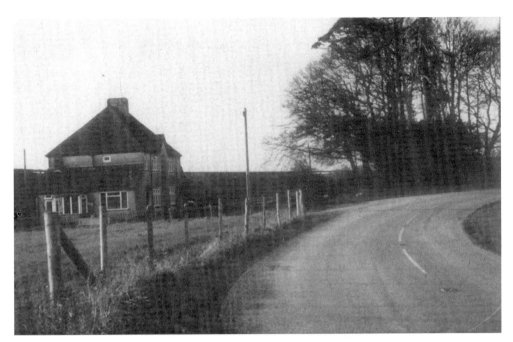

The road to North Fareham and Wallington. This is the start of Old Pook Lane, showing the two gamekeeper's cottages.

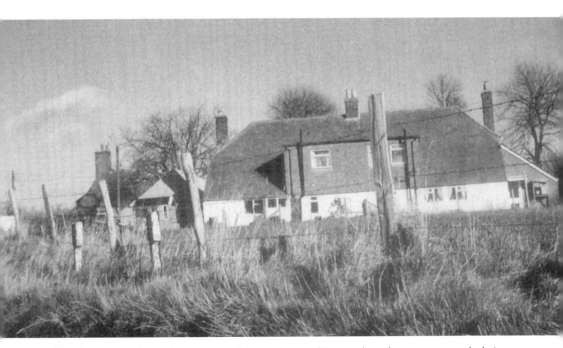

North Fareham situated at a dogleg on Pook Lane. Again, this must have been a crossroads, being joined by a footpath from the A32 and another (shown to the left of the fence) from Wallington.

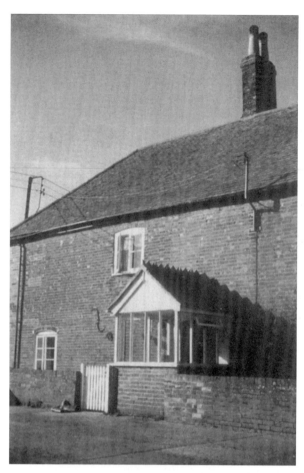

Left: This old house was once a pub. The landlord, Mr Webb, was fined for illegally selling beer during the time of church services; quote from a newspaper reporting on the incident, 'Where will this end ... ?'

Below: Old farm buildings at North Fareham. The settlement used to be much larger with many people working in Wallington.

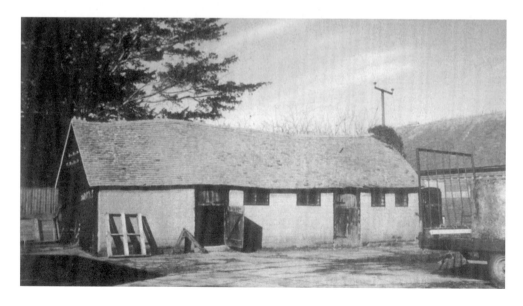

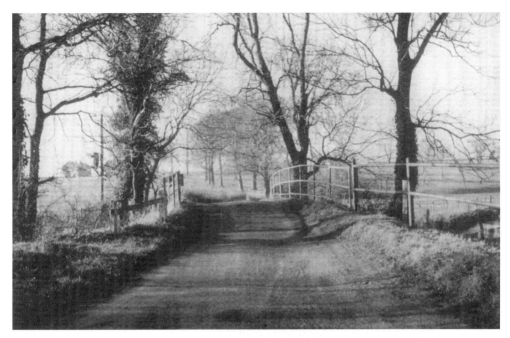

The bridge at Spurlings carrying the road from North Fareham. From North Fareham to the bridge, the road is narrow and sunk between high banks. It is one of the old roads which eventually leads to Boarhunt church.

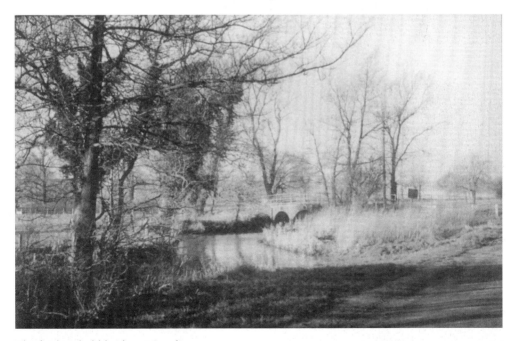

The ford and old bridge at Spurlings.

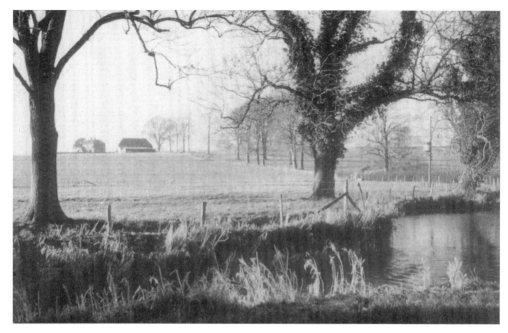

The River Wallington at Spurlings with part of North Fareham in the distance. The sunken lane is marked by a double row of trees.

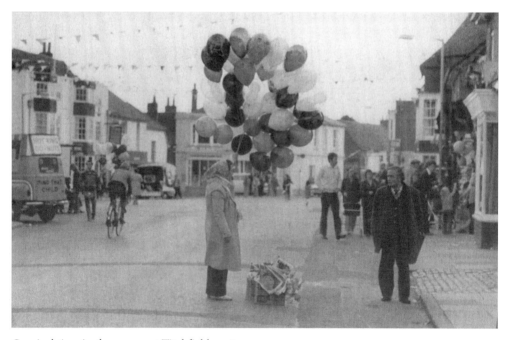

Carnival time in the square at Titchfield, 1981.

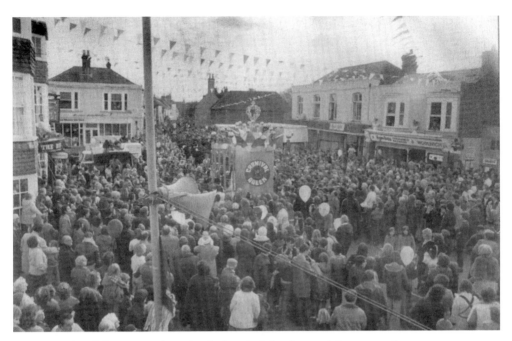

The carnival in full swing. Judging by the hoods, it has been raining as usual.

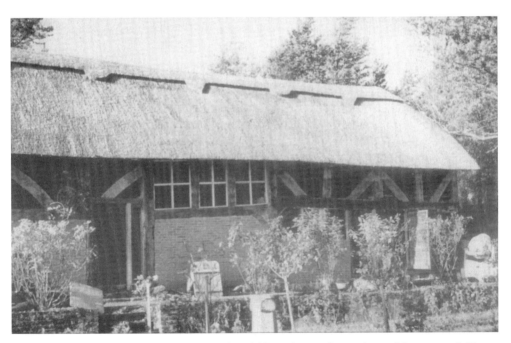

An unusually quiet spot in Segensworth. This old barn lies in the gardens of Segensworth House and was restored for Mr Gerry Day.

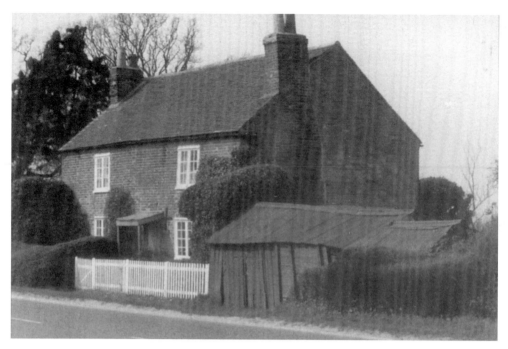

Newgate Lane. Old Newgate Cottage was the only building left standing when Fort Fareham was built. Its last owner was Mrs Bessie Parsons.

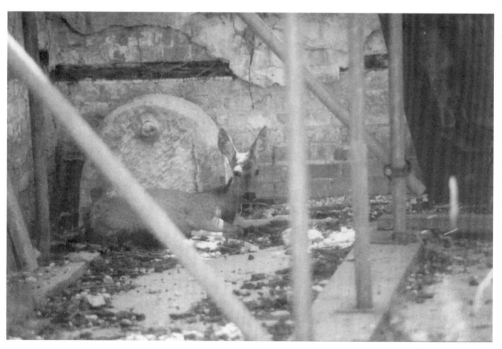

Cams Hall, 1991. A young deer lying in the shade on a very hot summer's day. It showed no fear when approached and allowed the photographer to pick it up and put it through a window gap.